T0328701

Cambridge Elements ≡

Elements in Politics and Communication
edited by
Stuart Soroka
University of California

DIGITAL TRANSFORMATIONS OF THE PUBLIC ARENA

Andreas Jungherr
University of Bamberg

Ralph Schroeder
University of Oxford

CAMBRIDGE
UNIVERSITY PRESS

CAMBRIDGE
UNIVERSITY PRESS

University Printing House, Cambridge CB2 8BS, United Kingdom

One Liberty Plaza, 20th Floor, New York, NY 10006, USA

477 Williamstown Road, Port Melbourne, VIC 3207, Australia

314–321, 3rd Floor, Plot 3, Splendor Forum, Jasola District Centre, New Delhi – 110025, India

103 Penang Road, #05–06/07, Visioncrest Commercial, Singapore 238467

Cambridge University Press is part of the University of Cambridge.

It furthers the University's mission by disseminating knowledge in the pursuit of education, learning, and research at the highest international levels of excellence.

www.cambridge.org
Information on this title: www.cambridge.org/9781009065542
DOI: 10.1017/9781009064484

© Andreas Jungherr and Ralph Schroeder 2021

First published 2021

A catalogue record for this publication is available from the British Library.

ISBN 978-1-009-06554-2 Paperback
ISSN 2633-9897 (online)
ISSN 2633-9889 (print)

Digital Transformations of the Public Arena

Elements in Politics and Communication

DOI: 10.1017/9781009064484
First published online: December 2021

Andreas Jungherr
University of Bamberg

Ralph Schroeder
University of Oxford

Author for correspondence: Andreas Jungherr, andreas.jungherr@uni-bamberg.de

Abstract: Digital technologies have changed the public arena, but there is little scholarly consensus about how they have done so. This Element lays out a new framework for the digitally mediated public arena by identifying structural changes and continuities with the pre-digital era. It examines three country cases – the United States, Germany, and China. In these countries and elsewhere, the emergence of new infrastructures such as search engines and social media platforms increasingly mediate and govern the visibility and reach of information, and thus reconfigure the transmission belt between citizens and political elites. This shift requires a rethinking of the workings and dysfunctions of the contemporary public arena and ways to improve it.

Keywords: public arena, political communication, sociology, conflict, geopolitics

ISBNs: 9781009065542 (PB), 9781009064484 (OC)
ISSNs: 2633-9897 (online), 2633-9889 (print)

Contents

1 Digital Transformations of the Public Arena

Look anywhere in the world today, and you see political discourses shifting. Governments, political elites, and news media find themselves challenged and their legitimacy questioned. New voices have emerged that sometimes contribute a more diverse set of viewpoints and opinions and sometimes expose societies' underbellies of exclusionary or reactionary beliefs and demands. Established news organizations are under massive economic pressure, which has not only reshaped the business of news but also its institutional and normative basis. At the same time, new sources of information have emerged that often do not conform to established journalistic norms of news production and that cater to groups that have formed around certain partisan issues or represent purely commercial interests. Furthermore, new types of private companies have become powerful conduits for the visibility and reach of information that are primarily in the business of selling ads by getting people to spend time on the platforms they provide and to socialize and share material there. In reshaping attention, they are tethering citizens and elites in new but potentially skewed ways. In short, digital media have thoroughly transformed our shared political information environment – the public arena.

These transformations of the public arena create wide-ranging but unfocused fears: digital media have allegedly pulled societies apart, allowed cunning politicians to manipulate a hapless public, given authoritarians unprecedented tools of social control, and destroyed a shared sense of social reality through rampant floods of misinformation. Many believe that digital media enabled the election of Donald Trump in 2016, supported the Brexit vote in the UK, strengthened the extreme right, and promoted COVID-19 denialism and anti-vaccine protests in Germany, while at the same time strengthening the authoritarian grip of Xi Jinping in China.

Examining these fears and diagnoses more closely shows that there is surprisingly thin evidence and little explanatory power to many of these analyses. Overall, digital media do not seem to tear societies apart by creating political homogeneous echo chambers or filter bubbles (Dubois & Blank 2018; Flaxman *et al.* 2016; Kitchens *et al.* 2020). While the informational quality in the public arena is increasingly contested – in view of the prominence given to partisan news organizations and to political elites that are comfortable in playing fast and loose with facts – this is not an exclusive feature of *digital* information environments. At the same time, proper disinformation via digital media is a marginal phenomenon with comparatively limited reach and dubious causal effects (Jungherr & Schroeder 2021). While the contemporary public arena clearly offers a stage for ambitious as well as haphazard attempts at manipulation of voters or foreign influence operations using digital media, the impact of these efforts on elections is much smaller than popular belief might suggest (Rid 2020). For example, we can explain the likely impact of media on the 2016 election of Donald Trump much more convincingly by looking at how his Twitter use translated into traditional media coverage thereby providing a broad stage for his populist ideas (Schroeder 2018a) and his open embrace or tacit acceptance of racist and ethnonationalistic ideas and groups (Bonikowski 2019; Gorski 2020). Even in authoritarian China, the fabled level of supposedly absolute digital control is more in the mind of propagandists or Western commentators rather than the reality on the ground (Stockmann 2020).

The unfortunate tendency to attribute every ill of contemporary society to digital media and in turn to reduce the discussion of digital media to the latest daily scare has done little for our understanding of the organization of contemporary political discourse and its institutional structures, a constellation we call the public arena. Make no mistake, digital media have deeply transformed these structures. This includes the transformation of the economics of news, weakening the traditional gatekeepers of politics and thereby enabling challengers, and the emergence of new actors that control digital infrastructures and so the reach and visibility of political information and public attention. But to understand these transformations, we must stop relying on singular cases of deviance or putative success and instead systematically examine the structures, functions, and continuities of the public arena. This also means taking a comparative stance and overcoming the relentless focus on isolated countries and cases. In practice, this means treating the United States and its enthusiasms and sorrows as only one specific, albeit comparable, case – especially as other constellations of the public arena may be less prone to temporary doldrums like those recently experienced there.

Hence we focus on the infrastructures of the public arena. What structures allow the publication, distribution, reception, and contestation of information that enable people to exercise their rights and duties as citizens? What structures allow elites to reach and to read publics in order to respond to grievances or demands? And how do digital media impact and transform these structures? Our argument is thus not predominantly about the quality of discourse or of content but about the structures that give space to and shape it. We take a comparative stance and analyze the transformation of public arenas in three different countries, each providing a different constellation of media, political, and economic systems: China, Germany, and the United States. This comparison highlights different ways in which digital media transform the public arena and the tensions in these systems. We argue that analyzing the public arena in this way is useful not just for understanding current tensions but also for developing suggestions to managing them more successfully.

We begin by presenting a definition of the public arena and charting its current transformation through new infrastructures. Building on this, we then present different constellations of the contemporary public arena in three instructive cases: China, Germany, and the United States. We close by previewing the role of the public arena in some emerging areas of conflict: solving financial crises, climate change, and the management of the COVID-19 pandemic.

2 The Public Arena: A Definition

Understanding contemporary politics is impossible without the concept of the public arena established through media. The structure of the mediated public arena shapes political discourses and consequently beliefs, the conditions of political competition, and the representation of social groups. As a consequence, the structural conditions of information environments, their transformations, and consequences are central objects of study for sociologists, communication scholars, and political scientists (Rauchfleisch 2017). The structures providing the environment for discourse, the public sphere, matter (Habermas 1962). But the recent structural transformation of communication spaces through digital media, their uses, and associated effects (Jungherr *et al.* 2020; Neuman 2016; Schroeder 2018b) makes it necessary to reconceptualize the public arena in order to account for its mediated nature and the subsequent consequences of shifts in media technology and audience behaviors. To do so, let us start with a definition of the *public arena*:

(1) The public arena consists of the media infrastructures that enable and constrain the publication, distribution, reception, and contestation of information that allow people to exercise their rights and duties as citizens.

(2) This excludes how people use these infrastructures for private life or for commercial purposes except when these uses come to bear on people's rights and duties as citizens.

(3) These infrastructures mediate the relation between citizens or civil society on the one hand and political elites or the state on the other.[1]

This definition focuses on the characteristics and boundedness of structures and how they enable and shape political discourses and political competition; in other words, discourses about questions of civic concern in non-private

---

[1] In the following, we use the pairings of citizens/political elites and civil societies/states interchangeably.

contexts. Our discussion focuses on technological and institutional aspects of infrastructures that allow the publication, distribution, and reception processes concerning political informedness. We follow Fraser (1990) in her argument that discourses in media and political communication are characterized by conflict as well as by cohesion. This contrasts with Habermas' conception with its normative dimension positing that the goal of political discourse should be agreement (Habermas 1962). That is why we use the term *arena* rather than *sphere* (Schroeder 2018b).

Academic discussion about the public sphere consists of various strands. We follow authors who focus on the structures of discourse and their influence on forms and determinants of rational discourse and its legitimacy (Habermas 1962) and the contestation of dominant discourses and discourse participants (Fraser 1990; Warner 2002). Again, we use the term public arena to emphasize the importance of contestation. We are mainly not concerned with the *quality* or *modes* of discourse but rather with the structures and transformations, including how infrastructures are regulated.

Today, as in the past, the public arena is primarily constituted by media infrastructures. In the past these were organizations and distribution networks for newspapers, television, or radio programs. Today this also includes digital media, "institutions and infrastructures that produce and distribute information encoded in binary code" (Jungherr *et al.* 2020: 7–8). This includes digital-born news sources, search engines, and other digital infrastructures providing spaces for connecting information producers with consumers without themselves producing informational content.[2]

Our analysis builds on the "media systems" approach by Hallin and Mancini (Hallin & Mancini 2004). We follow Hallin and Mancini in their emphasis of international comparison. Like news media, digital transformations of the public arena should vary between countries or regions depending on their histories and institutions. More specifically, to understand contemporary public arenas, we need to consider the opportunities and constraints of governments, transnational bodies, and civil societies to regulate and control infrastructures. This includes variations such as national regulatory traditions and how they influence internationally operating platform companies. For example, in highly market-based media systems like the United States, state actors experience

---

[2] Some of these digital media have become known as *platforms*. We prefer the broader term *infrastructures*. The latter term is broader than the term platform, which was originally linked to a very specific business model. But the term infrastructures allows us to include search engines and noncommercial digital media like Wikipedia. Nevertheless, we will also use the term platform in cases where digital media correspond to the platform business model, narrowly understood.

exceptional difficulties in regulating actors that provide the infrastructure of the transnational public arena. In contrast, actors in strong public broadcasting systems find this less of an issue. For actors in authoritarian systems, it is difficult to differentiate the state from media organizations in the first place, making regulatory interference comparatively easy. Hence too the technological foundations of the public arena can be similar while their effects on discourse vary as state actors have greater or lesser opportunities to shape communicative infrastructures.

Yet we also depart from Hallin and Mancini (2004). By focusing on system-level variables, Hallin and Mancini settle on an essentially static view of media systems and their constitutive features and consequences. As we will show, the contemporary public arena introduces new actors and new tensions between states, companies, and publics. A more differentiated view of grouping countries with shared conditions is needed, as is a more dynamic view of the continuous competition for influence among states and their civil societies, including in various macro-regions (Mann 1986; 2013; Mann & Riley 2006). Thus we focus less on eternal system-level conditions but instead on the transformations of the structures that constitute the public arena.

New Media Infrastructures and Their Impact on the Public Arena

Media infrastructures provide three functions in the public arena. They *produce information* that societies need to pursue the public good. This includes the coverage of events, actors, and societal conditions but also extends to a role as "watchdogs" by critically covering elites, institutions, and groups. They also *distribute information* by providing audiences access to it. And finally, they also make *participants visible to each other*. This last entails covering actions and views of elites or the public and providing opportunities for elites or the public to publish their views themselves. In turn, media infrastructures need to monetize or otherwise find support for providing these functions in the public arena.

In the past, organizations providing media infrastructures typically combined two of these functions – information production and distribution. A commercial newspaper – for example the *New York Times* – had within its organization a dedicated subunit for the production of information – the editorial desk. Other subunits within the same organization were tasked with running the distribution of the paper – such as the unit tasked with subscriber management or the unit tasked with organizing the logistics of getting the newspaper to points of sale. In other words, the same organization was tasked with information production and distribution for the public arena.

In today's public arena, this is different. While we still have organizations that produce, distribute, and monetize information – such as commercial news organizations or public broadcasters – there are also new media infrastructures that exclusively distribute information provided by others and monetize this distribution service. Examples include digital platforms like Facebook or Twitter that allow users to post links to content or others like Google that provide dedicated information aggregation services with previews to content by other sources. The popularity of these services means that they have become crucial for information producers to reach audiences, even if this means losing control of an important part of the distribution of their content and its monetization opportunities. This leads to a weakening of traditional media infrastructures and mechanisms to reach audiences. At the same time, there is uncertainty over the role in the public arena of these new distributional actors and what societies can reasonably expect from them or, if need be, demand from them through mandatory regulation.

Shifting Norms

In the past, the public arena predominantly relied on media infrastructures provided by journalism. This infrastructural role of journalism was supported by a shared set of institutional norms among media organizations and individual contributors. These norms included a shared code of impartial coverage of events, actors, and societal conditions, clear delineation between coverage and commentary, and standards of quality control in content production (Kovach & Rosenstiel 2021; McQuail 2013). These norms underpinned what journalism was supposed to achieve and they were institutionally maintained and transmitted. This allowed for public debate, critique, and contestation. This made clear what people could expect from media infrastructures and enabled challenging specific outlets or individuals if they were seen to be deviating from these norms. Of course these standards and norms were far from universally adhered to and contested, but that is beside the point. By providing a clear standard by which to measure specific behavior or content, journalism and its contribution to the public arena could be evaluated and legitimately criticized and provided the basis of an autonomous social institution. We can see the strength of these norms and their society-wide acceptance in a recent survey by the Reuters Institute Digital News Report (DNR). A broad majority of people – more than two-thirds in Germany and the United States – supported the ideas that news media should reflect a wide range of views and provide equal space to all sides. Over two-thirds among respondents in Germany also agreed that news media should remain neutral in debates while approximately half thought so in the United States (Robertson 2021, 41).

Nevertheless these norms focused on the production side of media infrastructures rather than the distribution side. In the past, this was not much of an issue. In organizations providing journalistic media infrastructures, the subunits tasked with information production were the units most closely connected to the ideational purpose of the organization, but other subunits like those tasked with the distribution of information by and large followed these ideational norms and goals. This is clearly not the case with new media infrastructures that are only concerned with the distribution of information. These infrastructures started out with goals and purposes clearly outside the scope of the public arena – such as the facilitation of interactions between friends and acquaintances in their private lives or an ill-defined "community" of users somehow independent of the public arena. But the growing popularity of these services and the extension of their use beyond people's private lives made them into important extensions of the infrastructures of the public arena. This shift of societal function and its attendant responsibilities is not yet internalized within these organizations and does not always fit well with their organizational culture. This is exacerbated by the fact that while the norms of journalism work well for organizations combining the functions of information production and distribution, they do not provide guidance for the challenges faced by organizations tasked with providing space for and distributing information provided by others.

At the same time, the institutional norms of journalism for information production have also been challenged from a different side: the norms of impartiality and separation of neutral coverage and opinionated commentary are not necessarily adhered to by new information providers in the digitally expanded public arena. Here, we find sources explicitly dedicated to providing explicitly partisan or even hyperpartisan coverage, sources funded by nonprofits or philanthropists supporting specific societal goals, sources exclusively following a for-profit logic that provide political content if it allows them to sell ads, and sources provided by volunteers dedicated to shared goals or issues. These diverse organizations and their staff follow different economic incentives and societal missions. Considering this, the role of journalism as advocacy in support of or opposition to political factions or societal goals has also grown in prominence among these new media organizations and young journalists (Agarwal & Barthel 2015; Eldridge 2018; Scott *et al.* 2019). As legacy news organizations adapt to the new business of news in digital environments and start to learn from digital-born competitors and hire from the pool of their contributors, conflicting views of the role of journalism have come to feature within these organizations (Wiedeman 2020). This normative shift away from media infrastructures committed to the goal, however imperfect, of impartiality in political and societal competition and toward open advocacy raises questions concerning their role in hosting, enabling, and adjudicating discourse and political competition in the public arena.

Rules of Access and Distribution

For media infrastructures predominantly concerned with the distribution of information produced by others – such as digital platforms like Facebook, Google News, Twitter, or YouTube – it is necessary to discuss different issues of governance from those that are first and foremost concerned with information production. In the past, the space for information in the public arena was limited by available column inches or broadcast minutes in the media infrastructures of its time. Today, the media infrastructures forming the public arena can accommodate virtually limitless information. There is little by way of scarcity of space but rather a scarcity of audience attention (Schroeder 2018b). This has led to the emergence of different selection criteria for different infrastructures. Organizations presiding over infrastructures with limited space select information based on its merits, such as being factually correct, being relevant to audiences, or conforming with specific rules of decorum (Shoemaker & Reese 2014). By contrast, organizations presiding over infrastructures with virtually unlimited information space principally allow all information access, except for information with negative characteristics – such as being illegal, harmful, or violating others' rights. Currently, the specific characteristics to include in this list of negative features are being negotiated. But overall, the consequence of this shift in selection mechanisms is that much more challenging, incorrect, and impolite content grabs attention in the public arena than when information was actively selected for its journalistic features or newsworthiness.

With the shift in prominence toward infrastructures with virtually unlimited space for information and mainly concerned with the distribution of information and not its production, the discussion about governance norms has come to be concerned with questions of access to distribution channels and amplification (Douek 2021; Gorwa 2019; Kaye 2019; Keller 2018a; Klonick 2018; Suzor 2019). The main issue is what *types of information, actors, or sources* should be allowed access to the public arena via digital infrastructures and what types should be prohibited. What types of information are *amplified or muted* and by what mechanisms? Does amplification follow algorithmic selection based on features or reactions, social curation through public interactions, dedicated editorial interventions by staff, or paid-for interventions foregrounding specific information for specific audiences? This is closely connected to the question of whether there are opportunities for *privileged partnerships* for selected actors, for example those of high societal repute or those willing to pay, offering them higher visibility or greater opportunities to selectively distribute information. Of course, the converse is also a challenge: which actors and sources to consistently *exclude*.

These decisions can happen on the level of a *piece of information/content* by determining its negative properties, for example by virtue of it being deemed illegal, potentially harmful, or violating others' rights. Or it can happen on the level of *actors or sources* based on their characteristics or behavior in the past. Or these decisions can be based on the *system level*, examining whether the composition of information streams conforms with normative goals such as balance or diversity. Access decisions can happen at the *point of publication* through automated or editorial checks according to the criteria listed above. Alternatively, decisions to revoke access can also happen *after publication* based on editorial decisions, social or automated filtering, or complaints. In all of this it is important for organizations running these infrastructures that there are clearly stated and publicly accessible internal *governance policies* and *transparency* about their application and the process underlying specific decisions. This allows people, elites, and competing organizations to contest specific decisions or, more generally, the underlying policies and processes. Suffice it to say that the current situation is very far from conforming with these requirements.

Negotiating Mutual Visibility

Media infrastructures also make people and elites mutually visible. For one, media infrastructures show elites to people and people to elites. At the same time, they also make people visible to each other. In the past, this surfacing of public opinion happened under strong editorial control by having peoples' voices feature in media coverage, allowing them space in interviews or letters to the editor, or aggregating them in statistics (Herbst 1993; Igo 2007). Today, people can take to social media to express their views, find others who share certain views, and be recognized by elites (McGregor 2019, 2020). This has beneficial consequences in surfacing unrecognized voices, injustices, or airing grievances. At the same time, these infrastructures also allow for nonmainstream but previously isolated voices to find and reinforce each other, thereby giving structure and coherence to radical movements and potentially contributing to the radicalization of individuals (Miller-Idriss 2020). Infrastructures also connect impolite voices directly with elites or groups and the individuals they are targeting. In the past, political speech was not necessarily polite and elites were in for a considerable amount of verbal abuse. Yet this remained confined to small gatherings and did not always reach those for whom it was intended. Today this is different. Impoliteness, hostility, or verbal abuse travels far, inspires imitation, and reaches its targets (Sobieraj 2020; Theocharis *et al.* 2016). Societies and media infrastructures have not yet found answers to these challenges of mutual and increased visibility in the public arena by negotiating the associated benefits and drawbacks.

International Reach

A further complication lies in the international nature of new media infrastructures (Kaye 2019; Schmidt & Cohen 2013). In the past, public arenas predominantly ran along national or language barriers according to the reach of their media infrastructures. Today, most countries' public arenas depend on media infrastructures that are run by organizations that have their origin and main seat in other countries – predominantly the United States. This introduces new tensions in the governance of these infrastructures. For one, there are geopolitical questions regarding the security of media infrastructures and foreign influence. Even more tricky are questions regarding the rules these international structures are supposed to follow. Do we expect a Western-based organization running an international media infrastructure to follow the laws and regulations of its home country, or change its functions to follow the laws and regulations of the specific country a user logs in from? Should a global set of internal governance rules that are applied globally be designed and followed, irrespective of the laws and regulations of any given country? In other words, should Google, Facebook, or Twitter treat every user as if they were based in the United States, or instead feel beholden to local rules and customs, or should they define a new set of international rules applicable to all?

The international role of media infrastructure introduces two important complications to the governance of the public arena. First, there is the issue of cultural dominance of media infrastructures provided by companies based in the United States or China for crucial elements of many countries' public arenas. The other, even thornier, issue is the role of these infrastructures in countries with more restrictive rights of free expression than the West. If one accepts the primacy of local laws and regulations for the governance of media infrastructures run by companies in foreign countries, this can make these companies complicit in restrictive measures by authoritarian governments. Do we then demand that companies based in Western democracies should leave countries that enforce laws and regulations that do not uphold variants of Western rights to free expression and personal rights? If so, then these media infrastructures cannot be made complicit in the pursuit of dissidents or users that fall foul of local regimes. Yet this would of course mean forgoing any increases in personal or societal freedoms these infrastructures might bring to authoritarian or transitional countries even if complying with local regulators or enforcement.

Similarly, Western societies must regard their current concerns about the unruly digital extension of the public arena and their associated demands for increased control in the context of the importance of exactly this unruliness in other international contexts. For example, while Western democracies were shocked by the sound and fury of the Capitol riots in Washington, DC on January 6, 2021 and answered them with demands for greater control over digital infrastructures and the exclusion of offenders, they also looked with sympathy on international political unrest against repressive regimes such as in Myanmar in 2021 and celebrated the role of digital infrastructures in enabling activists and demonstrators elsewhere. This leaves us with a dilemma: either we ask of media infrastructures to differentiate globally between "good" or "bad" unrest, one to be surfaced and amplified, the other to be silenced and its supporters de-platformed, or we must become comfortable with media infrastructures hosting content, views, and voices that, while remaining within legal boundaries, challenge certain global norms. Reacting to unruliness in the West with demands for greater control over the digital extension of the public arena could provide authoritarian governments with a pretext to do the same. This might turn out to be a bad trade-off, especially if Western episodes of unruliness might shock but remain far from having the potential to topple a democratically elected government or democratic regime, as was arguably the case with the Capitol riots in Washington, DC (Collins 2021).

These are questions emerging from the complication of the international reach of digital media infrastructures that feature various trade-offs and not one clear optimal choice and which therefore must be subjected to continuous observation and public negotiation within and between different societies.

These shifts in the workings of media infrastructures necessarily create tensions for the public arena. For one, we are potentially confronted with a much more diverse set of information sources that often challenge, for good or ill, the very institutions societies rely on. Public arenas now also must contend with a plethora of new, formerly (objectively or subjectively) unrepresented and openly partisan voices. Accordingly, they must navigate the resulting confusion, disunity, and diversity. Second, these voices do not all agree on what constitutes legitimate or constructive contributions or even the degree of civility, hostility, or truthfulness appropriate for the negotiation of the public good. And finally, these tensions in the public arena emerge when powerful actors, such as governments and the global companies running digital media infrastructures, negotiate the boundaries of free expression and control. This raises the stakes for the public arena and introduces variety into how different countries affect and are in turn affected by shifts in their public arenas.

3 Variations

Public arenas structure the limited attention space. How they do so is subject to the relations between states and civil societies as well as those between political elites and citizens. In the United States, the public arena is fragmented: there is a lively but incoherent sphere of contestation across various media where the dysfunctional politics of gridlock find expression and are fanned. Outside the two main parties and traditional media there are antistatist fringes and protest movements as well as well-funded interests that clamor to shape the agenda and leave the media just as incoherent as American politics is gridlocked. Even academic debate is subject to these dysfunctional dynamics. In China, the public arena is managed from above but also includes actors and sources that push against the party-state in protest or in an attempt at reform from below, and there is also contention among elite factions. Political discussion online is the liveliest part of the public arena, but remains within bounds, while the party-state measures online political expression in order to enable its responsiveness to civil society. In Germany, which we single out here as one case representing European media systems, there is still an orderly common ground in the media, contested by actors on the political fringes and those challenging the political status quo which, as in the United States, increasingly rely on their own media. The common ground in the German public arena therefore struggles with dissatisfaction around its edges. In all three cases, the public arena shapes attention spaces, which have become more differentiated and fractious.

A Fragmented Public Arena in a Fractured American Society

The role of digital technology in the United States has probably received more attention in scholarship than in all other countries combined. In recent years, research and media attention has focused on the activities of former president Donald Trump on Twitter, the importance of dis- and misinformation as amplified via digital media, and the effects of micro-targeting of audiences. Looking at these phenomena more closely, they are partly context-specific but also fit our arguments about the general workings of contemporary public arenas and their tensions. We can begin by foregrounding these tensions and how they find expression on digital media.

American society is riven with divides along economic, racial, rural versus urban, and religious lines. These tensions are not new; in fact, they can be seen as inherent features of American history and public life. Twenty years ago, Hall and Lindholm, dissecting a perennial trope in American debates summed up in their title, "Is America Breaking Apart?," pointed out that the public contestation of identities such as race or ethnicity, religion, and class are in fact a sign of national strength and resilience, allowing groups to express lines of societal conflict and collectively move toward compromise and social progress and reinforce national identity. The one exception, they noted, is race (Hall & Lindholm 1999, 144), a fissure that can only be overcome with an inclusive universalism that addresses the structural inequalities of racism (Schroeder 2020). And, as Campbell (a frequent co-author of Hall's) subsequently argued, in the last twenty years this national unity has been challenged and several new fissures have opened up and, exacerbated by the strategic choices of political elites, become more divisive (Campbell 2018).

To begin with, the Iraq War and the financial crisis, reinforcing already rising economic inequalities, put pressure on an already shrinking American middle class (Termin 2017) and reinforced the divides between the values of urban and rural communities (Cramer 2016). At the same time, growing economic pressure led to a deterioration of race relations and an increase in racial and ethnic tensions (Smith & King 2020). As a consequence, an ever-growing number of people and groups have felt excluded from the shared promise of the American Dream, one of the unifying forces so important for cohesion (Duina 2018). Further, the Republican Party – driven by fundamentalist fringe movements and special interests – settled on an obstructionist politics that when not in power aimed at cementing Republican influence through minority rule and so intensified the gridlock in national politics and increased the public's sense of frustration with Washington and politics in general (Blum 2020; Skocpol & Tervo 2020). In combination, these structural tensions have strengthened divisive political fault lines (Fiorina 2017; McCarty *et al.* 2016).

These tensions were important features in the election of Donald Trump as president in 2016 (Campbell 2018; Sides *et al.* 2018) and featured still in his loss in 2020. They are likely to continue to challenge American politics and provide massive roadblocks for a national government to find compromises and address the actual challenges facing American society. Finding similar structural tensions in the digital public arena is no surprise.

We can first focus on how these structural tensions find expression in American traditional media. Besides important and prominent centrist news organizations within strong media companies – such as ABC, CBS, and NBC – many news outlets exist that competitively cater to political partisan audience segments – such as CNN and MSNBC for Democrats and FoxNews for Republicans (Webster 2014). Similarly, newspaper journalism has become more comfortable in taking sides in political conflicts instead of pursuing objectivity (Lozada 2020). This has probably been exemplified most clearly in the internal conflicts within the *New York Times* and its coverage of the Trump presidency (Wiedeman 2020). Additionally, many digital news outlets emerged catering mainly to the political right with hyperpartisan news content that often bordered on misinformation (Bennett & Livingston 2021).

The drift toward a more fragmented media system is also due to market pressures that have made the news business highly vulnerable (Nielsen 2012). These pressures are felt by media organizations all over the world, but the United States, with its commercially oriented structure, is particularly vulnerable to this challenge. This vulnerability has led to calls for a publicly funded model for news media (Pickard 2020). Add to this the competition among news outlets such as the raucous fringes of talk radio and newer niche TV channels, plus online mobilization and alternative or partisan sites, and it becomes clear that the attention space of the mediated public arena is as fragmented as American politics and its economic and cultural divides.

In the contemporary public arena of the United States, it has become hard to identify a common agenda amidst the distractions of media coverage driven by scandal, the noisy moral outrage of extremism, the clamoring for visibility by protest movements and think tanks and lobbyist efforts, and the challenges to the impartiality of journalism from within the media system and from without. The dominant agendas of political parties are themselves contested with Democrat and Republican supporters no longer converging on or contesting the centre but continuously being drawn to political extremes of the spectrum by political activists, well-resourced lobbies, and interest groups. These internal conflicts within parties are given ample room in the media because partisanship and conflict generate audiences. At the same time, the general political agenda is still dominated by gridlocked national politics in Washington which, due in no small part to the internal struggles within the two parties, cannot be resolved by elite leadership or in a civil society where many groups feel unrepresented and there are growing divides. These fractured interests resonate in digital media where the competition to dominate the attention space and so the agenda adds to an already splintered public arena.

In this fragmented space with gridlocked agendas, digital infrastructures have evolved into powerful channels for reaching people. Platforms like Facebook, Twitter, or YouTube started out as outlets for people to exchange information but quickly evolved into spaces where people share media content publicly and privately. Over time this has made these platforms important distribution channels for traditional media outlets and for political elites to reach but also to monitor citizens. What started out as a process of social curation and amplification was soon commodified by platform companies through ad- and privileged-content programs, allowing media organizations and political actors to buy access to specific user subsets. Platforms thus enabled hyperpartisan media without established brands or audiences to reach people (Stier *et al.* 2020). This perceived contribution to the rise of highly contested political challengers, the opaque uses of algorithms in decisions about which information to display to whom, the aggressive business practices of platforms, and their lack of a coherent governance structure have all given rise to public fears and attempts at platform regulation (Napoli 2019). This increased scrutiny of the public arena will lead to more regulation from within and outside the United States and potentially curtail systems based on online ads.

Digital infrastructures are also important spaces for less visible underrepresented groups to form and in time spill over into the dominant public arena. Recent years have seen political groups with little access to traditional media or to established political structures forming counterpublics and contesting the political status quo and the media narrative (Freelon *et al.* 2020). The same mechanism also played an important role in the emergence of the American extreme right by giving attention to social media personalities and hyperpartisan outlets whose antics and agendas were picked up and amplified in legacy media coverage (Schroeder 2018a; Stier *et al.* 2020). At the same time, digital media offered important spaces for previously less visible social movements and protests, such as the coordination and "witnessing" in Black Lives Matter and protests especially in reaction to the police murder of George Floyd (Jackson *et al.* 2020; Meyer & Tarrow 2018; Richardson 2020). Here, digital media offer vital spaces of mutual support, information distribution, public documentation, and coordination for challenger movements that otherwise might not have access to enabling infrastructures (Jungherr *et al.* 2019b, 2021). Still, the highly fragmented public arena of the United States struggles to allow for sustained and focused attention that moves politics forward.

Digital media are an unruly attention space with highly uneven visibility and reach. At the same time, they are of crucial importance for challengers to the political status quo from different sides of the political spectrum to voice their opposition and to coordinate (Castells 2013). Here we should not forget that various elite actors – be it politicians from established political parties or journalists working at traditional news organizations – have clear incentives to exaggerate this unruliness for commercial purposes but also to legitimate their own position. A large amount of the current moral panic about the political effects of digital media in the United States is driven by the need for established elites to delegitimize their competition (Jungherr & Schroeder 2021).

In fact, the structural tensions discussed above force groups that are systematically underrepresented and actively excluded in elite institutions, politics, or in dominant media agendas – such as African Americans – to use the public arena to promote alternative agendas and coordinate. Only when this ongoing challenge finds expression in sudden and spectacular events, such as protests, does it manage to access media and thence political agendas. These challenges point to the lack of legitimacy of skewed elite representation and elite institutions in systematically under-representing certain groups as well as America's underlying and growing social divides. The American public arena is subject to these same fractures and remains an exceptionally fragmented attention space with a gridlock of conflicting agendas and highly unequal visibility and reach rather than a shared dominant agenda.

China's Struggle to Control a Segmented Public Arena

China is an authoritarian party-state. It might turn into a dictatorship if the party-state loses legitimacy and power becomes even more concentrated in the leadership. At the same time, the government enjoys high levels of legitimacy or support and has done so for many years (Kostka 2019; Whyte 2010). The current government's efforts to accelerate economic and societal development by means of taking the technological lead in digital infrastructure development is a continuation of a long historical tradition whereby the Chinese state has promoted very large-scale feats of engineering, primarily for agricultural irrigation, over thousands of years (Josephson 2005). Thus the political system has shaped – and been shaped by – a tradition of state-led mobilizing of technological and economic resources for building societal infrastructures. Another often overlooked feature of Chinese mediated politics is the high degree of protest and mobilization and expression, even if their visibility and reach remain within bounds.

An example can help here. When one of the authors asked a leading China scholar of the Internet about whether rural people, who get their news mainly from television – which is dominated by the official China Central Television – were disadvantaged because they do not have access to more diverse online sources, the reply was: Chinese rural folk watch the party's ritualistic national congresses (held every five years) mainly to look at the Rolex watches that party leaders wear and to laugh at how corrupt they are. Chinese citizens mainly support the state's goal for the media in keeping the public arena orderly – and especially its unruly online component. This orderliness also corresponds with official Leninist theory of the mobilizing function of media and it is compatible with the fact that citizens also have a great deal of skepticism toward the media and their rulers. In the West, the maintenance of order in China is seen as propaganda – correctly, from the point of view of societies where media are autonomous. But in China the role of the media also reflects a long-standing tradition whereby media mobilize civil society around common goals, goals that do not suit everyone. Thus, the attention space must keep various elite factions and discontented parts of civil society segmented and their expressions on media siloed – and this includes challenges to the legitimacy of the public arena.

Platforms are an increasingly central part of the media infrastructure. But in China, media have been governed by the Communist Party's conviction that they should serve the purpose of mobilizing the population or molding its political purpose. Labelling this exclusively as propaganda is misleading insofar as this idea of the role media play in society builds on the tradition of mobilizing the people behind the legitimacy of the emperor. Importantly, this tradition also demands of emperors that they must rule for the benefit of the people and that the people can petition and criticize them when they fall short. This Confucian tradition has recently experienced a revival, albeit influenced by the somewhat different Maoist tradition of "grassroots" or "mass line" mobilization (Tang 2016). In any event, the implication for media is that there is no autonomous media system as in high-income democracies. Instead, the public arena serves the party-state.

Yet this is also too simple: since the "opening up" of China under the leadership of former leader of the People's Republic of China Deng Xiaoping between 1978 and 1989, and especially since the 1990s, the media have become somewhat autonomous. This happened in two stages: first, commercialization (Stockmann 2013) followed by a second stage with digital media. These shifts have meant the growth and now dominance – at least in terms of audience share, though not necessarily of the political agenda – of private sector media. It has also led to the emergence of a vibrant digital part of the public arena, which has been less visible and has a bounded reach. This part of the public arena continuously challenges the dominant agendas of the party-state from the sidelines. While this is the arena in which the most lively and important political media activity takes place, it is kept within limits by the government. This activity originates from grassroots activism as well as from competing factions among political elites (or more precisely, limited factionalism within political elites plus high-profile politically relevant cultural and business figures.) While these cannot challenge the party-state's legitimacy or the public arena directly or in a coordinated way, they can do so indirectly, as well as serving as a weathervane that guides policy.

The party-state manages but does not entirely control this unruly part of the attention space. It cannot control it because it must accept market-led media for the sake of economic vibrancy, meeting the needs of media consumers, and for the sake of gauging citizens' or civil society's views and needs. By implication, its governance of platforms is at arm's length; the party-state curbs media where necessary but also otherwise allows them wide reign; an arrangement of semi-autonomy. We cannot know the precise arrangements of the governance or management of digital infrastructures (Wang 2020). One exception is basic knowledge about censorship of specific terms, such as the three T's (Tibet, Taiwan, and Tianamen) or other terms associated with controversial state action, such as Xinjiang, Uighurs, and Hong Kong. Various scholars are trying to crack this black box around censorship (Roberts 2018; Zhu & Fu 2020). Still, it is important not to make too much of this "black box." We do know the overall structural characteristics and tensions of the relationship between states and platforms whereby platforms need to be profitable and so maximize audience share (as in the US) while content distribution becomes problematic when it triggers the party-state's itchiness or during international public outcries thereby threatening profitability (outcries that also upset US platforms).

Some years ago, Rauchfleisch and Schäfer (2015) noted, against the conventional wisdom, that China had "multiple public spheres" on Weibo, then the most popular digital platform. One of these public spheres was even devoted to "meta-" discussions of the freedoms and boundaries of expression on Weibo. The Chinese public arena does indeed contain multitudes, but it can also be seen as a single mediated public arena, with semi- or limited autonomy maintained by segmentation and silo-ing. Its structure is split in a different way from the American one, pitting a less visible civil society including celebrity protest voices and elite spearheads with less reach and managed by the party-state on one side against a single non-fragmented media market competing for entertainment audiences on the other. Segmentation is also exacerbated in that the various subterranean forces cannot be channeled into a single visible agenda or into a single opposition party. But the politics within the state-shaped public arena are also split: supporting some elite factions over others or pitting local officials and their supporters against the central government and its agenda. Civil society and citizen groups can also be split, being officially recognized or not. In this way, visibility and attention to more and less contentious issues can be segmented while the public arena can serve at the same time to make the government aware, and to some extent accountable, in relation to various contentious issues.

China's public digital arena thus consists of sousveillance (Liu 2020), protest movements (Wright 2018), unofficial or registered (and so coopted) NGOs, other elements of civil society, which Palmer (2019) splits into different cultural groupings (religious, Maoist, and nationalist-modernizing), cultural and business celebrities with large social media followings, as well as citizen groups and activists and intellectuals. In this, it resembles other public arenas. Commercial media, including digital-born media, are similar to those in the United States and elsewhere inasmuch as a few players dominate. The crucial difference remains that in China the infrastructure these actors rely on is to a great extent nationally bounded, through technology as well as by means of law and regulation. But this control is far from universal, since many use VPNs and other workarounds. Still, the bounds of these solutions are nevertheless managed by the Great Firewall and the combination of legislation and technologies regulating the Internet domestically in China (Roberts 2018). Coming back to similarities, private sector companies providing digital technology and thereby infrastructures of the public arena compete fiercely in the Chinese and global market (Pan 2017; Stockmann & Luo 2017) and have succeeded on the basis of meeting consumer needs.

Cultural politics in China are also promoted within limits online, via entertainment, popular culture, and business and intellectual personalities. Celebrities and cultural elites are highly visible but also do not directly challenge the legitimacy of the party-state. Further, cultural soft power is also exercised abroad, more so driven by the party-state but otherwise not dissimilar from the soft power media foreign efforts of Western democracies and other large states.

Beyond this, the social credit system (SCS) features strongly in the discussion of China's public arena (Liang *et al.* 2018; Strittmatter 2018). It is another expression of Chinese attempts to control and incentivize people's behavior. As such it corresponds with the Chinese tradition of local policy experimentation (Heilmann 2008) and state-led efforts at digital economic development rather than providing the state with the all-powerful ability for surveillance, control, and interference with people's lives. Some of the more breathless Western accounts of an Orwellian all-controlling state are probably better understood as expression of Western anxieties about China than as an actual account of the reality on the ground. Still, the Chinese state's restrictive treatment of minorities, such as the Uyghurs, or local groups seen as challenging the central authority, such as protestors in Hong Kong, point to an increasingly nervous state jealously guarding its authority and cohesion. In this, digital surveillance and control of the public arena can play a powerful role.

The Chinese party-state seeks digitization above all for promoting economic growth and technological leadership. In this way the party-state can maintain its "performance legitimacy" (Zhao 2009). Hence there is a stand-off as market platforms and protest are accepted within limits. In its aim to maintain dual legitimacy in political and economic terms, the Chinese state resembles the United States and Europe, perhaps with a stronger awareness of the dangers of losing legitimacy outright and a greater emphasis on maintaining control. This duality is also where China and the rest of the world meet, on the geopolitical level of macro-regions (Mann 1986; 2013; Mann & Riley 2006), in seeking leadership in the competition for digital infrastructure development and markets, both for production and distribution, and consumption. Geopolitical competition, in turn, affects China's domestic economy, though the main effect on politics has been to rally Chinese public opinion to cry foul play by the West and to champion the efforts of its domestic technology companies.

In sum, China's segmented and siloed public arena is controlled by the party-state. This keeps attention, reach, and visibility compartmentalized and managed. This constellation reflects the tensions of an authoritarian party-state that must maintain legitimacy as an expanding foreign power and amidst globalizing markets, as well as keep the lid on an unruly domestic civil society.

Fractions around a Public Service Centre: Germany

Germany has often been cited as an example of a Northern European – corporatist – media system (Hallin & Mancini 2004). In this system, the media, and especially public service media, have a duty to represent diverse organized societal interests and some, like national newspapers, are aligned with these "corporatist" party interests (which also used to include, for example, the interests of unions, businesses, and regions).

Germany is part of the European Union (EU), a supra-national alliance of twenty-seven European member states founded on a core of Franco-German economic interests. The goal of this alliance was initially to avoid intra-European military conflicts through a higher degree of economic and political integration. Over time, it has morphed into achieving greater influence on the international stage through the combined weight of all EU member states. Member states coordinate joint policies in areas such as consumer protection, trade, the environment, finance, and security. Accordingly, rules and regulations in these joint policy areas are proposed, negotiated, and decided within EU institutions and implemented by all member states. While regulatory efforts are thus often supra-national, public discussion and the contestation of political issues remain firmly within national boundaries. This, and the domination of a few technocratic EU bodies strongly influenced by Germany and France, has given rise to a growing disconnect between European-level policy making and national-level politics and an associated democratic deficit of EU policies quite apart from its institutions.

The public arena in European countries is partly shaped by American platform companies. Google is the search engine of choice while Facebook, Twitter, YouTube, and WhatsApp are by far the most important services for posting, sharing, and commenting. While some national media brands have developed popular apps that serve as specific points of entry into news (such as Bild, Der Spiegel, or Tagesschau in Germany), the fact that parts of the European public rely on – and in turn might be influenced by – US-based companies has raised concerns in the EU in relation to national and local media organizations.

Northern European media systems like Germany are characterized by a mix of strong publicly funded television and radio broadcasters plus strong national commercial newspapers (Kuhn & Nielsen 2014). While there is competition to set the agenda between the two, combined, they provide Germans with balanced political coverage and information. Recently, this status quo has come under attack in parts of Europe. For example, governments in Poland and Hungary have strengthened their control over public service media while at the same time putting pressure on private news organizations that limit their freedom and funding. At the same time, challengers in more liberal European democracies, such as Austria, Germany, and Switzerland routinely challenge public broadcasters, claiming that their coverage does not adequately cover the breadth of the agenda by excluding their positions, a challenge increasingly manifest in digital media. This can be seen in the European far and extreme right's increasing reliance on digital media to develop an alternative information space, providing audiences with information in direct conflict with those presented in established news media (Guhl *et al.* 2020).

Beyond the news media, civil society also garners visibility on digital media. Here, until recently, Facebook was paramount while Twitter was mainly a tool for agenda building and setting, which made it into a space popular among journalists, academics, politicians, and public intellectuals. Recent criticisms of Facebook as a driver of hate speech and promoter of extremist challengers have led to increased regulatory attention within and outside the company on deviant users, behavior, and content. Consequently, some challengers have moved to other channels such as Parler, Telegram, WhatsApp, or YouTube. Comment sections of prominent news media provide an additional space for public contestation (Toepfl & Piwoni 2018). The multitude and opaqueness of how these services operate makes it difficult to assess the size of these challenges and their popularity or reach. There are many studies that are deeply instructive on specific cases but fail to offer evidence about their total reach or effects on users – a situation that also applies to the United States and China. This opaqueness can be used both by political challengers and their critics to exaggerate their visibility and the threats posed to democracy.

In Germany, digital media have long served activists as a successful extension of the public arena. Be it in the online mobilization around protests, such as during the protests against the infrastructure project Stuttgart 21 in 2010

(Jungherr & Jürgens 2014), in discursive interventions, such as the feminist grassroots campaign #aufschrei in 2013 (Drüeke & Zobl 2016), or in the establishment of new political parties, such as the German branch of the Pirate Party (Bieber & Leggewie 2012), digital media have served activists as powerful spaces to share information, coordinate, and document the strength and importance of their cause to a wider public. In these cases, activists and progressive groups took to digital media. While the German far and extreme right have also used digital media for many years, it took the refugee "crisis" of 2015/16 to create a broad alternative digital information environment on the political right that reached beyond the narrow confines of far and extreme right supporters. During the refugee "crisis," established news media were challenged by large parts of the public as to whether they were indeed reporting impartially about the events or whether they were withholding or misrepresenting facts in order not to endanger the societal support for what were seen as the government's generous policies toward refugees (Haller 2017). While these challenges turned out to be largely unfounded (Maurer *et al.* 2019), they increased the reach of the alternative digital information environment of the political right far beyond their core constituency (Guhl *et al.* 2020; Haller & Holt 2019; Heft *et al.* 2021; Rauchfleisch & Kaiser 2020b; Stier *et al.* 2017). This unruly extension of the public arena continuously provided the space for alternative narratives that challenged the accounts of traditional media as well as space for people holding these views to find each other and to coordinate protests. Politically, the new party Alternative für Deutschland (Alternative for Germany) profited from and fanned these activities and gave a platform for these views (Gäbler 2018). Similar infrastructures and sources came back to prominence in 2020/21 among skeptics and opponents of the government's responses to the COVID-19 pandemic (Guhl & Gerster 2020). While the fortunes and relative importance of Germany's digital extension to the public arena have waxed and waned in response to the salience of external events, its infrastructures and sources have proven persistent over many years and exhibited a surprising flexibility in terms of specific topics and policies on which they challenge Germany's political center.

It is no surprise then to find the EU and national governments in Europe attempting to control public arenas by means of regulation. Examples are copyright regulations and regulations that seek to curb hate speech and personal attacks online by shifting responsibility on to digital media companies for online speech, such as the German Network Enforcement Act (NetzDG) (Gorwa 2021). While well-intentioned, these initiatives risk shifting the governance function of what constitutes legitimate political speech onto private companies, predominantly based in the United States, and away from European or national institutions (Strossen 2018). Additionally, these attempts lead to a further entrenchment of current market leaders as only they can afford the legal wherewithal and technical infrastructure that allow them to comply with an ever increasing amount of locally varying legislation.

The extension of the public arena to digital media has led to a partial loss of control by traditional gatekeepers such as news media and political elites. Positions have surfaced that are far off the otherwise accepted opinion spectrum. Examples include personal attacks on politicians and journalists, the rhetoric of political extremists and far-right populists, and anti-science and conspiracy claims in opposition to state interventions to stop the spread of the coronavirus. These fractious publics openly contest the legitimacy of established political elites, the government, and news media. Not surprisingly, established political elites and news media challenge the legitimacy of the claims made by fractious publics, often in fact contesting the validity of expression via digital media and their contribution to the public arena overall. In the strongly public service–centric public arenas in Germany and elsewhere in Europe, we see attacks on this centre by fractious publics that fall outside of an elite dominated consensus. This raises challenges for containing visibility and attention within a well-ordered public arena. More specifically, providing outsiders with a line of attack on the status quo causes problems for how US-based platforms operate in Europe. The attention space of this public arena is dominated by the tensions between strong publicly funded and well-established commercial media companies on one side and digitally enabled challengers to their authority and coverage on the other.

4 Tensions

Challenging Gatekeepers

One of the most important questions in the discussion of the contemporary public arena is the role of gatekeepers. In the past, these actors guarded access to the public arena. Elite news organizations decided which information or actors reached mass audiences by selecting which news items to run or to feature prominently (Shoemaker & Vos 2009). Political organizations, such as parties, decided which political positions were viable in political competition and which candidates or agendas to feature prominently (Cohen *et al.* 2008). In doing so, these institutions had considerable control in deciding which information, political positions, politicians, or policy options made it into the public arena. By shaping access, they also shaped the space of political options for discussion on matters of common interest. While this might have excluded information, positions, or actors critical of the status quo, it provided the public arena with established rules and boundaries.

The contrast with the contemporary public arena is stark. Digital media have extended the set of actors who can push information into the public arena by providing new access options, including personal blogs and social media profiles. They have also given rise to new digital-born news outlets that contribute to the public arena with a variety of standpoints for many niches. There are digital-born outlets that are run for commercial or partisan reasons and others that provide non-profit news or fact-checking services. Digital media have thus extended the variety of norms and business models for actors who cover and decide what is news (Konieczna 2018; Usher 2017). On top of this, news media outlets increasingly rely on digital platforms, such as Facebook or Twitter, to connect them with audiences (Nielsen & Ganter 2018). This makes these companies into powerful new gatekeepers whose internal governance remains opaque, including the workings of their algorithms and how they shape users' information environments. At the same time, this has led to a weakening of power over the mechanics of informational reach for traditional news providers that, in the past, controlled the function of news provision and of distribution. Finally, digital media have undermined the financial basis for commercial news production and distribution by transforming the ad business and shifting major revenue streams from news organizations to digital infra-structures such as Google (Nielsen 2012). These trends have meant traditional gatekeepers can be bypassed and have given rise to much soul-searching about their current function and business models.

Political organizations have fared little better than news media in their role as gatekeepers to the public arena. Digital media have provided challengers to established parties and the political status quo with tools for coordination, organization, and resource generation. This has given rise to new advocacy organizations but also ad hoc movements – such as #metoo, #occupywallstreet, or #blacklivesmatter – with varying interest in institution-building or policy follow-through. Issue-driven activism is particularly prominent in the American context but competes in an attention space crowded with activist movements and agendas in a fragmented and log-jammed political system. As Emirbayer and Desmond put it, "publicity itself can be highly consequential, while social movements, for their part, can result only in modest change" (Emirbayer & Desmond 2015: 215). This relative lack of coherent institutional change in light of massive attention-grabbing digital media events threatens to translate among activists into a growing sense of fatalism (Gurri 2018).

The function of gatekeepers in controlling access can also be described as a refereeing function for the attention space. Media organizations not only present information or provide political actors with access to their audiences; they also elaborate, contrast, or comment on information. By doing so, they adjudicate the factualness of information or statements, the viability of proposed alternatives, and the legitimacy of positions. As a consequence, important news organizations are consistently attacked by political challengers or incumbents for the factualness of their coverage and the legitimacy of their commentary (Sehl *et al.* 2020). Recently, this challenge has been crystallized in the terms of "fake news" in the United States or "Lügenpresse" (lying press) in Germany, while in China "rumors" challenging government and media accounts are widespread (Huang 2017).

In the contemporary public arena, this gatekeeping role has been extended to digital platforms, though with fewer established rules. In becoming referees, these digital platforms have been increasingly forced into a position of adjudicating or sanctioning their users. In the tempestuous public arena, especially in the United States, this has led to de-platforming actors that are thought to maliciously pollute the public arena, such as controversial self-declared media outlets like Alex Jones' Infowars, or social media accounts linked to foreign influence operations aimed at disrupting and delegitimizing political discourse, and recently even former US president Donald Trump. The build-up of controversy about the role of digital platforms in the perceived deterioration of the public arena between 2016 and 2020 forced the companies hosting them – partially at least, and for better or worse – to accept the role of referees in political competition. Not surprisingly, this has given rise to criticisms, including by both parties in the United States. These criticisms have also featured prominently in legacy media concerning the legitimacy of these decisions and claims that digital platforms were putting their thumbs on the scale of political competition. These claims have intensified as the transparency of platforms' refereeing decisions remain opaque not only to content but also with regard to more foundational infrastructural elements such as payment processing or hosting opportunities, without which consistent contribution to the public arena becomes untenable.

While it has been fashionable to diagnose a death of gatekeepers for the contemporary public arena, it is more fitting to speak of their weakening. It is true that they have lost some capacity to control access to the public arena, but gatekeepers still set the agenda and amplify information and legitimize government. It may be that candidates can post a controversial, provocative, or scandalous tweet, but for this to reach mass audiences or to set the agenda it still needs the endorsement of news organizations with large audiences. Fringe candidates can capture wings of a party or start and maintain their own organization, but to win significant and lasting electoral success or influence policy they still need the sponsorship of large and settled political organizations.

The emergence of Donald Trump between 2015 and 2016 as a viable candidate for the US presidency is an example of the cooptation of traditional gatekeepers by challengers. Trump began his candidacy as an outsider in a broad field of candidates for the nomination of the Republican Party. Neither Republican nor media elites saw him as a promising or even legitimate candidate. Still, his shrewd use of media appearances and his continuous courting of scandal by breaking taboos guaranteed high viewership and readership figures for anyone covering him and his campaign. Ratings-dependent networks identified this feature of his campaign early on, which led to high media attention and continuous coverage of his campaign from the beginning, even by networks who tended to cover him and his position critically, such as CNN. As then chairman of CBS Leslie Moonves stated on Donald Trump's candidacy: "It may not be good for America, but it's damn good for CBS" (Bond 2016). So while news organizations, their editors, and journalists initially baulked, they still covered Trump and his antics excessively – after all, in a highly commercial media system, there is strong competition for audience attention – so enabling him to gain a dominant presence in the public arena at a time when neither his standing in the polls nor his policy proposals would have merited coverage following traditional news values. Thus, at a point in the primary campaign when news organizations in the past could have exercised their gatekeeping power, Trump's ability to attract audiences created a codependency between him and the news media. This robbed Trump's competition for the presidency of the visibility they needed and ensured, combined with the support of a populist-leaning electorate, a successful primary campaign (Schroeder 2018a). The commercial weakness of traditional gatekeepers made the media complicit in a challenge to the political status quo.

Similarly, the Republican Party, after some early resistance, allowed Trump to become its figurehead and provided him with the support he needed (Levitsky & Ziblatt 2018). Again, the reason was instrumental. In 2016, the Republican Party faced demographic change of the American electorate and was thus open to a political outsider with a platform of "white identity" (Jardina 2019) or "white protectionist" (Smith & King 2020) populism. Once in power, the Republican administration pushed for populist policy options on immigration and a takeover of important institutions such as the Supreme Court, and through a compromised census provided the basis for advantageous redistricting of voting, hence potentially offsetting demographic disadvantages in elections to come. Again, a weakened traditional gatekeeping organization, the Republican Party, was coopted by an outsider, Trump, who in the past would have been excluded from the public arena and political competition. At the same time, this weakness benefited the outsider. First, by recognizing a pre-existing but not party-politically recognized populist agenda in the American public (Claggett *et al.* 2014), Trump now brought these voters into the fold of the Republican coalition. Then, once in office, Trump proved a willing conduit for the realization of long-held policy preferences and institutional changes pursued by fringe groups aligned with the Republican party, such as the Christian Right or the Federalist Society, that prior party leaders chose not to pursue (Skocpol & Tervo 2020).

The disruption and contestation of the public arena by political outsiders is contingent on the weakness of traditional gatekeepers and, in the American case, the dependence of news organizations on commercial viability. Further, a fragmented political system, where the highest office is subject to a majoritarian contest, can be vulnerable to challengers; the case of Narendra Modi in India, whose rise in the face of traditional media and his own party's establishment, partly using Twitter as a megaphone, provides a similar example (Schroeder 2018b). Episodes like the enabling of Donald Trump in 2016 through mass media and the Republican Party were not a deterministic outcome but one in which specific openings for participants in the public arena, including the electorate, led to their shared responsibility and cooptation into Trump's victory and agenda.

This makes it important not to focus exclusively on the United States. In Germany, the public arena is dominated by news coverage by public broadcasters, ARD and ZDF, and a small set of highly influential commercial national newspapers. The tradition of serving the public and representing different interests is strong among all of these organisations: politically, both public broadcasters and commercial newspapers are aligned with positions represented by the parties in Germany's political mainstream and represent the viewpoints across this spectrum.

In view of strong competition in this market and in the range of represented positions, to date it has not been possible for alternative news organizations to emerge beyond niche positions. Nor have there been successful challenges to these traditional organizations over a prolonged period, even though a party realignment has taken place that could have shaken up this media landscape. Yet the role of these traditional media organizations as gatekeepers to the German public arena is still very strong. This does not mean that they are not challenged. Crucially, public broadcasters in Germany face a shift in audience behavior, particularly facing challenges in attracting young audiences to their linear news programs. Accordingly, a shift to nonlinear formats and mobile platforms – like Tagesschau, a very popular mobile news app by Germany's public broadcaster ARD – is of crucial importance in remaining relevant in public discourse and justifying their fees. But the public broadcasters also face more general political challenges. For example, during the European refugee "crisis" of 2015/16, German media were routinely challenged, and not just by Germany's far right, for allegedly covering the topic in a consistently biased light in favor of refugees and the government. This challenge has been shown to be factually ill-founded (Maurer *et al.* 2019) but was and is still highly influential and has weakened the perception of public broadcasters as unbiased sources of information (Eimeren *et al.* 2017). More recently, German public broadcasters have come under fire by critics of Germany's policy interventions in reaction to the COVID-19 pandemic. These repeated attacks on public broadcasters and important newspapers risks weakening the public perception of their legitimacy as unbiased gate-keepers and referees of the public arena. The persistence of this threat seems yet unrecognized by these organizations, and looking at the state of the American public arena, this negligence is worrisome.

The role of gatekeepers is stronger still when we turn to the Chinese public arena. The Chinese state still exercises strong influences on the editorial deci-sions of Chinese news organizations (Stockmann 2013). News organizations have to some degree extended the bounds of allowable topics and criticism of – especially local – government officials. Yet this has not been a story of uni-directional progress toward greater freedom in a restricted space. Instead, it resembles more a back-and-forth between newspaper editors and state censors in which phases of an enlarged space of critical coverage are followed by stronger restrictions (Osnos 2014), with Xi Jinping swinging the pendulum toward greater restrictions. Established gatekeepers, in this case the state censors and news organizations, still dominate the Chinese public arena. Nevertheless, specific digital media have evolved into spaces where challenges to official accounts and the coverage of news organizations can emerge (Stockmann *et al.* 2020). In China, digital media are subject to the interventions by censors or the government (King *et al.* 2017; Roberts 2018). This means that challenges in the attention space depend on party elites picking up on them and thus legitimizing them or the state allowing them to persist. Most protest movements are therefore kept locally segmented or constrained to issues that do not undermine the party-state. One example of protest that has been more generally tolerated, as Wright has argued (Wright 2018), is nationalist – or what could also be termed "ultranationalist" populist (Schroeder 2020) – protest since it has mostly suited the government. In contrast, the visibility of other competing party elite factions and their supporters (including ultranationalists when they have gone too far) has been curbed, entirely or in tone or vociferousness, since it potentially challenges the party-state's use of the traditional media for maintaining order.

In all three constellations, the public arena faces a shift in the role of gatekeepers. The role of traditional gatekeepers in governing the reach and visibility of political information, shaping public political attention, and refereeing political competition has weakened, be it through the emergence of alternative sources or tools that provide publics with opportunities for information distribution and coordination, or challenges to their economic foundations. At the same time, we see the legitimacy of gatekeepers challenged. Combined, the structural transformations of the public arena have led to a reconfiguration of gatekeepers and contestation of their legitimate functioning.

Shaping the Limited Attention Space

As digital media have expanded and reshaped access to the public arena and weakened the influence of gatekeepers, the main issue in analyzing these arenas is not one of access but of visibility and reach (Jungherr *et al.* 2020). By expanding the amount and diversity of information available at any one time on any one topic, digital media have transformed the struggle for attention within a limited attention space (Schroeder 2018b). Public arenas allow for the emergence, contestation, and setting of political agendas. Agendas establish the topics that political elites and media and sometimes parts of civil society identify as most important or pressing (McCombs 2014). Pluralism and inclusiveness are necessary for the emergence of agendas that truly reflect the concerns and demands in a society. This reflection is threatened if agendas are dominated, for example, by a few central institutions such as a select set of news organizations. In this case a dominant agenda may be favored that closely mirrors the interests and balance among political, business, and media elites. If, on the other hand, there are many competing news organizations with different business models and ideological proclivities and a lot of opportunities for civil society to have its voices heard, dominant agendas can be circumvented. However, this second constellation of the public arena, as we shall see, benefits political challengers more than incumbents (Jungherr *et al.* 2019b).

An important characteristic of the contemporary public arena is increased information and communication density. Traditional news organizations pick up stories from digital or partisan news outlets; journalists, political elites, and organizations listen closely and react to attention shifts on social media platforms (Karpf 2016; McGregor 2020); while social media users comment and contest media coverage and the statements of political elites (Jungherr 2014). It comes as no surprise then to find news and political agendas to be more interconnected (Gilardi *et al.* 2021; Harder *et al.* 2017; Neuman *et al.* 2014; Posegga & Jungherr 2019; Vargo *et al.* 2018). But the shaping of attention is complicated and causal influences remain opaque as researchers often only have access to incomplete or partial snapshots of the attention space or of visibility in different areas of the public arena, which makes it difficult to pinpoint the structure of influence (Jungherr *et al.* 2019a).

What seems clear, though, is that participants in the contemporary public arena are increasingly tethered to each other (Schroeder 2018b). For example, automated listening tools surface actual or staged points of contention among social media users. This makes opinions and their supposed strengths visible to elites, to journalists, and to social media users themselves. Digital media have thus become a highly influential source through which social and political reality gets mediated and acted upon. This is troubling as digital media only provide a deeply skewed reflection of reality driven by their biased user populations, usage conventions, motives, and the code underlying each service (Jungherr *et al.* 2016). Still, the skewed nature of these reflections is predominately ignored in their analysis by political elites (McGregor 2020), journalists (McGregor 2019), and academics (Theocharis & Jungherr 2021) alike.

At the same time politically interested audiences are deeply tethered to news by constant must-know updates by trusted news sources on their phone, social media channels, or their email inbox and their own trusted circle through social media and messenger apps. This is likely to contribute to a sense of heightened awareness of partisan conflict (Settle 2018).

The largely unreflected biases that politicians and journalists find themselves tethered to matters even more once we think about the reactions they directly receive through their social media profiles or which they can access through social listening tools or practices. If it is true that only a highly involved subsection of the population comments actively on digital media concerning politics, then we can also expect to find the viewpoints of the more polarized parts of society expressed there. This means that by listening actively to voices expressed on social media, politicians and journalists focus increasingly on polarized and extreme viewpoints, voices, and reactions to their initiatives, legislative actions, or articles. Over time, political and journalistic elites will thus develop a distorted picture of political and social realities and adapt their behaviors and positions accordingly. Through this mechanism, mutual tethering through digital media might thus contribute to an increased sense of unbridgeable differences in society.

The increased mutual tethering among participants in the public arena has added a new feature to the selection and amplification of topics worthy of attention. Traditionally, it was the role of editors of news media to select newsworthy information and feature it in their outlets. These top-down selection decisions followed journalistic norms and brand identity. Today, these decisions to feature stories in the news are important but additional processes determine which information gets amplified algorithmically and socially on digital platforms. This has added an element of insecurity about the trustworthiness of information for audiences. Trust in news has been shown to be strongly associated with familiarity with brands as well as stylistic and presentational factors. But news encountered on online platforms that typically have opaque selection and amplification rules and decontextualize specific news stories appears to be connected with higher levels of skepticism (Toff *et al.* 2021).

The limited space of attention in today's public arena is thus shaped by a combination of top-down editorial decisions and interventions by political elites, plus bottom-up processes whereby social interactions with information items contribute to their visibility among media and political elites, as well as, furthermore, algorithms that automate decisions about the display and amplification of attention based on content characteristics, sources, and interaction patterns in the service of profitable advertising revenue.

Especially the last of these shaping patterns has given rise to much controversy among the public and in academia (Diakopoulos 2019; Napoli 2019). Putting our trust in algorithms for automated production, distribution, and amplification decisions makes for uncertainty, especially as this trust remains blind since the exact working, consequences, and reach of the algorithmic shaping of the public arena remain unknown. Academics cannot get access to the necessary data, which are proprietary. Marketers and platform companies have access to the data, but they are not concerned with the workings or potential dysfunctions of the public arena. This knowledge gap has led to much speculation about how algorithms distort the public arena.

Hence we have to approach the question of the current influence of algorithmic decision making on the public arena indirectly: two shifts have taken place. One is from traditional media to online ones, the other from desktop to mobile. Both shifts have entailed more algorithmic shaping, and both have brought a number of fears: filter bubbles, polarization, dis- and mis-information by malicious or unwitting actors, greater commodification of the lifeworld, and more. Underlying these fears is a common account made in news media and among the public that young people get news differently from older generations and therefore are more at risk of being digitally manipulated, that most people get most of their news and political information online, and that much reception of online news and political information is politically polarized. Testing these expectations is complicated, not the least because usage patterns, platforms, and access devices constantly shift and researchers have only incomplete access to data documenting actual behaviors and effects. Nevertheless, looking at the available evidence indicates that they might be overblown.

For example, it might be thought that younger generations have different sources of news than the older generations. But as Taneja *et al.* (2018) have shown for the United States, comparing the top twenty sources of online news, there is hardly any difference between these groups. Additionally, several of the top twenty sources are well-established "brands" such as the major television and cable news channels and major quality national newspapers such as the *New York Times* and the *Washington Post.* Nor was there a particular political skew in the patterns of online news consumption within or between the two generations.

Second, and again for the United States, we can simply quote the top-level findings of Allen *et al.* (2020):

> First, news consumption of any sort is heavily outweighed by other forms of media consumption, comprising at most 14.2% of Americans' daily media diets. Second, to the extent that Americans do consume news, it is overwhelmingly from television, which accounts for roughly five times as much as news consumption as online.

This shows that news encountered in algorithmically shaped information environments is a relatively minor phenomenon compared with other non-algorithmically curated access points to news and as a share of all algorithmically curated information.

Finally, according to Yang *et al.* (2020), more than half of American Internet users do not consume online news, but more importantly, observed over a five-year time window in the shift from desktop to mobile news sources, mainstream media online still provide the "common ground where ideologically diverse audiences converge online." Similar patterns have been shown in Germany (Scharkow *et al.* 2020). In other words, accessing news through highly algorithmically curated forms of access, such as mobile devices, does not automatically lead to a loss of the informational center of news.

A different way to examine the prominence of mainstream, digital-born, and partisan or alternative news sources online is to examine offline and online audience share more closely. The Reuters Institute Digital News Report (DNR) allows the direct comparison between the sixteen news brands with the greatest reach through traditional channels (TV, radio, and print) and those with the greatest online reach for the United States and Germany (Newman *et al.* 2021: 113). In the United States the two lists are very similar, nearly all the news sources with the largest traditional reach are also among the most prominent online sources. Only local radio news, PBS news, regional or local newspapers, and the *Rush Limbaugh Show* are missing. Conversely, we only find four new brands among the most prominent online news sources – BuzzFeed News, Huffington Post, MSN News, and Yahoo! News. This shows that even in the United States, traditional news brands remain dominant in online environments. Looking at DNR data from the year before shows that the partisan digital news outlets that dominate the public debate about the dangers of alternative news sites online – such as Breitbart, The Blaze, or the Daily Caller – had a weekly reach between 7 percent and 5 percent audience share (Newman *et al.* 2020: 88). This is an important reminder that these hyperpartisan outlets only have a relatively small audience share.

In Germany, we seemingly find greater differences between the news brands with the greatest reach through traditional means and online. But looking closely shows that while the sources with the greatest reach deviate, brands among the top sixteen online but not among the traditional sixteen are the digital editions of important legacy media brands – such as FAZ.net, Stern.de, Sueddeutsche.de, and Zeit.online. The only exclusively digital news sources are news aggregators run by popular providers of free email services – such as gmx.de, t-online, and web.de (Newman *et al.* 2021: 81). Again, we find the online news environment dominated by legacy media brands. The top "alternative" or "partisan" sites have an even smaller audience share than in the United States, with Tichys Einblick (4 percent) and three smaller sites at 2 percent in the top five (Newman *et al.* 2020: 71).

It is more difficult to obtain comparable data for China, but the Chinese Academy of Social Sciences reports that 77.25 percent of online news consumption is via WeChat, a mobile app, with Tiktok (39.02 percent) in second place among other platforms like Weibo and Toutiao, while online TV (6.06 percent) and newspapers/magazines (0.68 percent) are far behind. In other words, a gulf has opened in a mobile-centric society between online and offline, which makes party control of content, via the government's close collaboration with platforms, of central importance in shaping a dominant or shared news agenda. The legitimation of the party's goals and how it mobilizes society behind them is counterposed by segmented spaces of commercial and online media that it must control. These findings can be complemented by the extent to which mobile phones have become central to urban and rural people in China (Yan & Schroeder 2020), even as, on the national level, legacy media still set the agenda.

Stepping back from our three cases shows a common picture. In all cases the public arena has been extended to include added online spaces of attention. This can be beneficial – as in the case of citizen journalists, independent fact checkers, or digital-born news organizations providing access to a broader and deeper spectrum of news. This extension can also be detrimental, by providing access to hyperpartisan news, extremist content, or purposefully or accidentally misleading visibility for issues or actors. At the same time, the degree to which this has complicated agendas in the public arena varies between our cases. Systems with predominantly commercially financed news, such as in the United States, appear to be highly vulnerable to fragmentation, while systems with publicly funded news organizations, like in Germany, appear to be much more stable, while still being subject to fractiousness. Even in China, the extension of the public arena increases visibility to challenges but gives them less prominence because of a more segmented and managed attention space compared to democracies.

Perhaps a key problem in the current debate is that the rush to examine new spaces of attention and visibility has somewhat obscured the extent to which continuities persist. For example, the degree to which political agendas are still dominated by attention to certain dominant political actors, positions, events, or agendas is often overlooked. This is true for both elites and citizens, even if new forms of connectedness and visibility provide somewhat enlarged venues and somewhat more differentiated avenues for both sides to shape dominant agendas. Nevertheless, these new venues and avenues have enabled new challenger political positions to gain a foothold, including positions that question the very legitimacy of various media channels, both of legacy media and of digital or social media. Another reason for obscuring these continuities is that algorithmic shaping of information provision has been mystified. Too many exaggerated claims and fears persist even though the process by which companies try to maximize profits is rather banal: through specific tailoring and targeting of information, companies hope to maximize "engagement" and attention. While evocative, the exact relative benefits of these procedures remain undocumented and conversely, so does the empirical evidence for the suspected associated democratic harms.

Governing Visibility and Reach

Public arenas shape the reach and visibility of information (Jungherr *et al.* 2020) and attention (Schroeder 2018b). Technological shifts have regularly been accompanied by strong expectations for their effect on the public arena – be it the telegraph, newspapers, radio and television broadcasting, and the Internet and digital media (Bimber 2003). New technologies do indeed provide shifting usage incentives and opportunities for individuals – such as opportunities for information choice, publication of original content by individuals without support of mass media or elite institutions, and the formation of networked publics. They also influence the conditions under which institutions of the public arena must act – such as the economic conditions of commercial news media and the attention economy among public intellectuals and academics.

The growing prominence of digital platforms has led to their entanglement with various social forces and thereby risen to the attention of regulators (Gorwa 2019). In this regard, they resemble the dynamics of all new large technological systems or infrastructures, which eventually become frozen once they are increasingly shaped by social forces (Hughes 1983). But regulating the role of platforms and how they shape visibility and reach in the public arena has been difficult since regulatory approaches are still mainly based on past approaches to the regulation of media organizations (Fukuyama & Grotto 2020). At the same time, digital platforms themselves struggle internally with establishing reliable governance rules and procedures in order to retain public acceptance and to signal to regulators that they are trying to keep their shop clean on their own in order to avoid too much government oversight (Douek 2019).

There are obvious differences between the United States, Europe, and China regarding media regulation. China has tight control of media (Stockmann 2013) and platforms (Stockmann *et al.* 2020). The party-state has close collaborative relationships with platform companies. While the details of these relationships are opaque, their overall aim is to maintain the legitimacy of the party-state and to enable it to gauge public dissatisfaction and keep expression within well-managed bounds. Hence the common image of Orwellian control and manipulation of public opinion in China is misleading; instead, the public arena is lively and there are multiple public spheres (Rauchfleisch & Schäfer 2015), which give extensive room to protest and contention (Wright 2019). Some protest and contention are tolerated more than are others as they allow the party-state to be responsive at various levels of government, especially local government. But this responsiveness remains within bounds in suppressing fundamental challenges to the legitimacy or stability of the party-state. Such fundamental challenges are also not desired by most citizens, who support the government in keeping the digital public arena, which has become riddled particularly with unreliable commercial actors, safe and orderly.

Europe and the United States differ regarding media regulation, with Northern Europe having strong traditions of public service media and therefore extensive regulatory input. In contrast, the United States relies much more on commercial broadcasters and has less state-led regulatory input (Hallin & Mancini 2004). This approach has also shaped the approach to the self-regulation of digital media (Fukuyama & Grotto 2020). But regulating the digital infrastructures of the public arena is not just a question of degree, it is also a question of state capacity (Pan 2017) at a time of intensifying geopolitical competition.

While European regulators are increasingly wary of the reliance of their national public arenas on American companies, as of the time of this writing, they have not yet found a satisfactory way to address their concerns and those of their citizens. These concerns have given rise to regulatory initiatives on the national and EU levels whereby interest groups and governments have tried to tilt the balance toward their national or EU-wide news and media industries and against their US-based competitors. One of the most prominent initiatives is the German *Leistungsschutzrecht für Presseverleger* (ancillary copyright legislation for press publishers) that has sought compensation for German media organisations from digital platforms that provide links previewing their proprietary content. Most efforts to regulate US-based platform companies, however, have been situated at the EU level. The most prominent conflicts between the EU and platform companies include questions of taxation and competition, privacy and data protection (Farrell & Newman 2019a; Keller 2018b), and freedom of expression versus individuals' defamation rights and hate speech (Kaye 2019). The regulatory ambitions on the side of the EU have increased and the most heated rhetoric in these matters has shifted toward looming trade wars between the EU and the United States.

For the EU and its member states, the general conundrum remains that its public arena crucially depends on infrastructures developed, managed, and hosted in another country with different legal traditions, sensibilities, and potentially divergent economic and political interests. So how do the EU and its member states ensure that its legal tradition, economic interests, and political processes find expression in the governance of digital infrastructures that shape the reach and visibility of attention on their territory and avoid being turned into de-facto vassals of the US legal and economic system via the conduct of these platforms? The crucial importance of digital media for reach and visibility has pushed this conflict to the fore and given rise to demands for so-called "digital sovereignty" in Europe (Pohle & Thiel 2020).

The most prominent question in current discussions about regulating the public arena is content moderation and its consequences for political speech (Gorwa *et al.* 2020; Kaye 2019; Keller 2018a). The election of Donald Trump in 2016 and his supporters' conduct on digital media during his presidency have raised concerns about the impact of intentional disinformation or violent and harmful speech on the democratic process (Bennett & Livingston 2021). While the actual effects of disinformation on democracy have been overblown (Jungherr & Schroeder 2021), the harm they cause on the individual level with impoliteness, hate speech, and downright harassment is considerable.

The venom directed at politicians (Theocharis *et al.* 2016) and journalists (Waisbord 2020) often focuses especially on women and minorities, threatening to silence their voice and representation in discourse (Sobieraj 2020). It is no surprise then to find digital platforms and regulators have started to pay more attention to political speech online and its governance as well as the protection of people who find themselves the target of digital harassment.

At the same time, there is a danger that an indiscriminate extension of liability can lead to detrimental effects, such as excessive moderation of political content by platforms, which may curtail political speech, or the entrenchment of market leaders that are able to shoulder the resource burden of broad content moderation (Keller 2018a; Strossen 2018). Recently, alternatives to the deletion of problematic political content have been tested and put forward. For one, Twitter used labels indicating factually contested content in tweets in the context of the 2020 US presidential election and prompted users to confirm if they really wanted to retweet content, thereby creating friction and slowing the spread of political information in general. This intervention, although comparatively mild, seems to have created the hoped-for effects.

In view of the steady increase of content on digital platforms, dedicated moderation decisions for individual items of content are de facto no longer possible. Hence automated and algorithmic moderating decisions, which work probabilistically, have been proposed. Here, an extended public and legal debate is needed about the consequences for political speech and about the transparency decisions necessary to ensure their legitimacy (Douek 2021; Gorwa *et al.* 2020).

In general, greater control over an increasingly unruly public arena might seem desirable. Yet it is important to keep in mind the detrimental effects. Increased moderation of controversial political speech could have negative unintended consequences. For one, moderation of political content depends on broadly shared agreement about what constitutes political facts or misrepresentations. The degree of agreement is likely to vary between topics and media systems. For example, it is likely that a topic of hard empirical facts – such as the legitimate processing of votes in an election – can be established, at least in countries with strong political institutions and independent news organizations. Accordingly, a platform can fact check, label, or take down content contradicting institutionally established facts. A topic carrying more uncertainty – such as the harms caused by (as opposed to the reality of) climate change – is much less likely to be able to be fact-checked in the same way. The same goes for topics for which the factual basis is still evolving. Take certain aspects of the Covid-19 pandemic for example: if digital platforms in March 2020 would have followed the World Health Organization in their advice on the use of masks to stop the spread of the virus, they would have had to take down or label as misleading all content by users advising the use of masks. As topics carrying great uncertainty are likely to feature strongly as objects of political conflict, it is unclear how moderation and labelling of content will prove feasible. Similarly, the establishment of even hard empirical facts in countries with weak, factionally controlled, or corrupt political institutions and no independent news organizations will also prove challenging. Yet, these are the political systems that are also most likely affected by the spread of unverified or misleading political information.

In any case, moderation depends on the acceptance among those moderated. Yet people tend to be unruly and the governed develop tactics to work around the rules set for them. Similar avoidance mechanisms can be expected for digital platforms. For example, recent research by Daniela Stockmann shows that even in China, a country with comparatively strong control of digital platforms, users develop ingenious workarounds of censorship rules and retain a surprising ability to share information and coordinate (Stockmann 2020). If this is true for China, the chances to effectively control the more unruly publics in Western democracies, on platforms more remote from the regulators' grip, appear rather slim.

Even more problematically, moderating the evidence (however obnoxious) of social and political conflict out of sight does not solve the underlying conflicts themselves (Strossen 2018). Thus, communities that are moderated against will detach themselves from the public arena and shift to spaces out of sight of the public arena in order to provide visibility for topics and to reach supporters (Keller 2018a). This means that they can still coordinate and perhaps become more radicalized through isolation and/or not being confronted in debate. Among recent examples are moves to the Parler platform among the far right in the United States or the widespread use of Telegram during the protests against coronavirus restrictions in Germany. At the same time, evidence on de-platforming decisions against the far-right on YouTube between 2018/19 shows that these decisions reduced their ability to reach large audiences (Rauchfleisch & Kaiser 2021). The power of companies to deny access to the public arena via digital infrastructures of the public arena became broadly visible in the de-platforming of Donald Trump and far-right actors in the aftermath of the Capitol riots in January 2021. This decision clearly reduced their ability to influence the news agenda and their reach to large audiences. Yet the ad hoc nature of this decision by a few heads of platform companies is troubling and showcases their influence over who has a voice in the public arena. Hopefully this dilemma inspires a sustained and balanced discussion about the rule-based, transparent, and contestable governance of who gets denied access to the public arena through these platforms and why. In any case, heavy-handed moderation or de-platforming of selected actors is seldom as straightforward a solution as it seems (Zuckerman & Rajendra-Nicolucci 2021).

It is also important to consider that the current discussion about the governance of public arenas predominantly focuses on the moderation of text or static images. Moderation of video clips, live video streams, or audio is much more demanding, be it with regard to manual checking or computational analysis. Beyond this, even thornier issues await. For example, the growing use of gaming and virtual reality environments for entertainment and shared events can potentially become part of political information exchange and coordination. The variety of content and speech formats and contexts available via gaming spaces and virtual reality environments, combined with the potential reach to mass audiences, provides a new set of challenges for the governance of public arenas.

Going beyond content, governance also applies to the provision of the infrastructure of information, coordination, or organization. Here, many companies provide newly formed groups and actors with the infrastructure for hosting, internal communication, or the processing of payments. These companies thus enable additional actors or groups to participate in public arenas. Should these companies therefore also follow digital platforms in their moderation of speech and decline service to actors or groups that have become controversial for actions on platforms not necessarily connected with their own service; in other words, de-platform them? Early examples include the denial of advertisement opportunities and use of services for Alex Jones' Infowars website. While there is little reason to feel sad about the exit of Infowars from the US public arena, the provision or decline of services of controversial participants in public arenas is a thorny one, which cannot be approached by means of ad hoc decisions.

Yet another area where regulators in the United States and Europe are starting to pressure companies that provide infrastructures for the contemporary public arena concerns their exercise of market powers to avoid and suppress competition. Antitrust regulation is a powerful force for regulation. At the time of writing Amazon, Facebook, and Google face strong legal challenges regarding alleged abuse of their market power. The impact of these proceedings can be considerable, as the effects of the antitrust action of US Congress and the European Commission against Microsoft in the late 1990s and early 2000s has shown. Underestimating the potential impact of regulators' attention can therefore heavily impact the resources and abilities of even the strongest companies. As in the case of the moderation of political speech, a stronger regulatory grip appears to have little downside at first glance, but this might neglect unintended downstream effects. Here, the question is whether the public arena really gains from breaking up its infrastructure providers and having them therefore fracture into a myriad of different services, with different rules, different audiences, and different cultures. In other words, what would we gain from a breakup of the public arena by losing the few remaining channels that allow information distribution and focus attention centrally, like Facebook?

Challenges thus abound in the governance of the public arena. Therefore, we should not expect public arenas to converge in the near future on a more orderly and less contested solution. On a more general level, this discussion shows the asymmetric relations between states that host digital platforms such as the United States (for high-income democracies) and China (a potential model for low-income and weak democracies or authoritarian societies). The United States has influence over others because of the ownership of platforms: economic, ideational, and surveillance capabilities become US-dominated through widespread international adoption of its infrastructures and its laws, culture, and interests. The geopolitics of platforms, including Chinese ones, are unavoidable.

The Geopolitics of Public Arenas

The discussion about public arenas often focuses on their national characteristics: for example, the topics of discourse, political agendas, political competition, or user behavior. But as we have seen in the previous sections, contemporary public arenas also demand a wider perspective. Public arenas are in fact an increasingly important element in geopolitics. This takes two forms: first, there is the question of cross-border influence operations in the public arena of a different state; second, we must consider the role of technological infrastructures that enable visibility and shape the attention in a national public arena but that are developed, maintained, and governed in another. The importance of both aspects has become ever more apparent in recent years.

While the public arena was traditionally confined to national infrastructures (such as national or local newspapers and parties and political organizations), broadcast media (such as radio and television) could send information and opinion across national boundaries. Not surprisingly, looking back we find many attempts by governments to influence public opinion in competing or allied states through targeted information and opinion infusion in the public arena through dedicated broadcast media. Examples include the Nazis targeting the US public through dedicated English-speaking radio broadcasts aimed at reducing the public support for the war effort; Radio Free Europe, a radio station located in Munich, financed by the US Congress, targeting Eastern European states under Soviet influence during the Cold War; or television newscasts from West Germany, reaching across the inner German border and watched illegally by people in the DDR, the so called *Westfernsehen* (West TV).

These attempts at shaping the attention space of public arenas of other states naturally continue in the digital age. Famously, in the aftermath of the US presidential election of 2016, attempts by Russia to influence the campaign and exacerbate structural tensions in US civil society were prominently discussed. Yet, given the rather limited scale and reach of these efforts and their surprisingly amateurish design, their influence on the actual results can safely be assumed to be marginal. Foreign influence operations remain of course part of the international playbook of geopolitics and therefore warrant the careful attention of security agencies and secret services (Rid 2020). But their actual impact may lie less in the clandestine manipulation of public arenas but rather in surprisingly open interventions. For example, the television station Russia Today is financed by the Russian state and runs dedicated branches for Germany, the United Kingdom, and the United States. Especially in Germany, its coverage has been repeatedly linked with positions that give disproportional space to Germany's far-right, Euro-skeptics, anti-government voices, and critics of the government's pandemic measures (Bensmann *et al.* 2020; Kohrs 2017; Weiß 2017). At the same time, Russia has also been shown to financially support far-right parties and their candidates across Europe, such as France's Front National (Gatehouse 2017), or Germany's Alternative für Deutschland (Der Spiegel Staff 2019). These interferences are likely much more impactful than a few ill-financed Facebook and Google ads, and happen in plain sight.

Beyond these targeted interventions, there are other ways public arenas influence each other across borders. For one, American soft power has found expression in its cultural influence in Western Europe, with its consumer offerings of popular entertainment and a recent fascination with American politics. The international obsession with Donald Trump introduced citizens of Western democracies to the intricacies of the American voting system to a degree they would be hard pressed to replicate for their own national voting systems. This influence and continuous focus also led agenda items to travel between countries. One example was the declarations of international solidarity in reaction to the police murder of George Floyd and the subsequent protests in the United States. Protests went global and erupted in countries with varying levels of prior anti-racist activism, such as France, Germany, and the United Kingdom. The respective public arenas started addressing the issue of local structural racism in reaction to events in the United States even when the respective contexts were quite different. The agenda item therefore travelled across borders via digital media. Here, the consistent international focus on social media trends, habits, or memes facilitates the transmission of politically relevant agenda items along non-traditional infrastructures of the public arena.

Geopolitics also comes into play in an even more direct way. In the past, national governments had direct control, access, and knowledge of the infrastructures constituting the public arena. Printers, newspaper distribution hubs, or broadcasting stations were on national territory and could be controlled, if necessary, while at the same time foreign interference could be minimized or prohibited. In the contemporary public arena, the distribution channels are shifting and becoming more opaque and remote. This means that governments and societies have relinquished control over crucial elements of the public arena. This is exacerbated by distribution infrastructures developed, hosted, and controlled in the United States or China, which raises doubts regarding the integrity or security of the public arena in other countries whose populations have come to rely on these infrastructures. Accordingly, there are geopolitical conflicts over the use of digital media or infrastructure controlled by countries in competing macro-regions.

The United States is the country with the strongest international influence on infrastructures of the public arena. It hosts the most important companies providing hardware (e.g. Amazon, Apple, Intel, and Nvidia), software (e.g. Microsoft), and services (e.g. Facebook, Google, or Twitter) that provide the backbone for the public arenas of many countries. This gives the United States and US-based companies influence in the public arenas of foreign countries. The question of potential influence on foreign citizens has been consciously neglected in the discussion of the opportunities provided by digital technology, as proponents emphasized a digital world devoid of the interests of governments. This changed in 2013 after Edward Snowden, an IT professional working for the NSA contractor Booz Allen Hamilton, stole and published a massive trove of documents detailing the extensive spying practices of the US government through digital technology and the cooperation of leading US-based companies. The subsequent NSA scandal has established the question of the security of infrastructures based, developed, or controlled in the United States centrally in the discussion of the governance and security of contemporary public arenas.

The United States itself appears to be aware of the risks of relying on technological infrastructures provided by competing countries. This can be seen in its treatment of hardware, software, and services provided by Chinese firms. The most visible case of growing tensions is Huawei, a privately held telecommunications company based in China. Crucially, it is an important provider of telecommunications infrastructure, such as 4G telecommunications networks all over the world, and a strong competitor for the provision of new 5G networks. The United States has led a campaign against Huawei achieving an even stronger market position internationally by stopping its acquisition of US companies, incentivized US telecoms operators to stop cooperating with Huawei, leaned on allies – such as Australia, Germany, and the United Kingdom – to exclude Huawei from bidding to provide new, local 5G telecommunications infrastructures. The reasons given are US security concerns that Huawei's infrastructure could be used by the Chinese government to spy on governments, companies, and citizens. Similar arguments have been raised regarding popular social media platforms, such as TikTok and WeChat, or the production of chips and hardware on Chinese territory. While these claims are contested and seen by some as a pretext for the United States to wage a trade war and protect local companies, they illustrate the growing concern in the United States over a dependency on technology from abroad.

China is also aware of the influence of foreign companies and governments in the contemporary public arena. Famously, China hosts the most strongly controlled and simultaneously most highly developed public arena. Behind the Great Firewall only Chinese companies are allowed to provide infrastructures for the public arena in an unfettered way that allows Chinese users to exchange information, coordinate market activity, and engage in leisure activities. Accordingly, the Chinese public arena is shaped by companies that are separate from – and differently governed than – the public arena in most Western democracies, which are dominated by US companies. Chinese users search the digital public arena with Baidu, they chat on Weibo, and participate in market transactions on Alibaba. This media infrastructure is vibrant and its functionality and degree of integration in society far ahead of Western democracies. But Chinese elites are also aware that China is far from self-sufficient. For example, US sanctions on chip makers willing to provide Huawei with hardware necessary for its products sharply illustrated how deeply dependent even China is on collaboration with the United States. It comes as no surprise then that Xi Jinping declared Chinese technological self-sufficiency a vital developmental goal.

The Chinese approach to data law beyond its borders is likely to continue to generate comment and produce tensions. China's policy of cybersovereignty entails territorial control over data infrastructure domestically, but it is also trying to promote this approach when extending this infrastructure along the Digital Silk Road or to other developing nations. This sovereignty principle is not so much "imposed" abroad as diffused to "receiving" countries since companies increasingly accept the costs and pursue the benefits of complying with data localization. Erie and Streinz (2021) call this the "Beijing effect," whereby China shapes data laws and data infrastructure beyond its borders. Erie and Streinz observe that countries increasingly rely on digital infrastructure supplied by Chinese corporations and suggest that these countries might emulate elements of Chinese data law when adapting them locally.

We would argue that this happens elsewhere too, but in a different way: one example is the General Data Protection Regulation (GDPR), an expression of the "Brussels effect" (Bradford 2020) whereby non-EU states adapt their laws in consideration of GDPR. Unlike this "Brussels effect," whereby governance converges toward an "optimum" solution based on the aims of furthering rights, the "Beijing effect" operates via push and pull factors for data governance along the Digital Silk Road. But such an extension into the international order also applies to the United States (the "Silicon Valley effect"), whereby the laws that govern US digital infrastructure are being diffusely promoted as transnational ways of favoring American companies and their rules for the Internet.

Europe faces the same challenges as the United States and China regarding the risks of relying on foreign-controlled infrastructure, yet without having access to homemade alternatives of competitive quality. This situation is exacerbated through the increasingly heated competition between the United States and China. On the one hand, Europe must avoid exclusive reliance on US infrastructures. Reliance on the United States would risk having to accept US governance over infrastructures and the attention space of their public arenas and at the same time perpetuate the security risks that were so clearly illustrated by the NSA affair. At the same time, the increased international tensions between the United States and China concerning human rights abuses and digital surveillance capabilities mean that Europe cannot simply shift its dependency to Chinese technology and software. One approach the EU has taken is to increase regulatory ambition and efforts toward US-based companies. Examples for this are the Digital Services Act (DSA), Digital Markets Act (DMA), and the Data Governance Act (DGA).

While the prolonged tug of war between the EU and the United States for the governance of digital technology continues (Farrell & Newman 2019a), the question remains how long the EU can fall back on declaring rules for foreign technology without providing viable alternatives. Over time it is unlikely that the EU can mobilize the necessary technological and regulatory skill set to design efficient rules without being able to consult local experts from academia and business whose expertise crucially depends on having access to cutting-edge technology and data. The current imbalance is only bound to increase once artificial intelligence becomes even more central in the technological infrastructures of the public arena. Current privacy and data regulation in the EU make it unfeasible for researchers and industry to stay abreast of current developments and thus they risk falling irrevocably behind business practices, platform technology, and the impacts of governance initiatives. There also remains the question of public support of restrictive techno-logical regulation when tensions mount or benefits are at stake.

In general, this discussion has shown how strongly the geopolitics of macro-regions (Mann 1986; 2013; Mann & Riley 2006) matter in the contemporary public arena. Accordingly, questions of dependencies and influence will continue to loom large. But we can come back to our earlier point: these geopolitics follow and express tensions and mutual dependencies that are inherent in the dynamic of large cross-national technological systems and do so in distinctive ways for our three cases.

Questioning the Legitimacy of the Public Arena

The struggle for legitimacy is a constant feature of public arenas. Political competitors regularly contest each other's legitimacy in choosing tactics or proposing solutions and sometimes, but especially in times of social conflict and uncertainty, they do so by challenging the legitimacy of gatekeepers – most often, the news media. One such conflict has arisen with political challengers in Western democracies that have regularly attacked the legitimacy of established parties and the news media. In Europe, this phenomenon has become manifest in regular attacks on public broadcasters from the political right (Sehl *et al.* 2020). Claims of politically motivated, biased, and misleading coverage are often connected with demands for defunding public broadcasters, as seen in Switzerland in 2018 or the ongoing struggle over license fees and leadership of the United Kingdom's BBC. The exact nature of the challenges of perceived biases in media coverage follow the main social and political cleavages at the time. For example, in the United Kingdom, the challenge of biased coverage hit the BBC from the political right, which claimed the BBC was favoring view-points of cosmopolitan, continental, and City of London elites. At the same time the political left attacked the BBC, since it felt the broadcaster was not challen-ging factually wrong or misleading claims by Brexit campaigners, with regard to its coverage of the Brexit referendum. Similarly in Germany, the public broadcasters have recently faced strong attacks. In 2016, they were criticized for their coverage of the refugee "crisis" in 2016 by the far right, who claimed they were purposefully suppressing information indicative of the supposed dangers of immigration. During the COVID-19 pandemic of 2020/21, public broadcasters were attacked again, this time by a coalition of coronavirus-skeptics, deniers, and the far right for supposedly uncritically cheering on government policies that restricted public life and the movement of people in order to stop the spread of the virus, and for stoking supposedly unfounded fears of the virus.

But the United States is the country where the challenge of news media by elected officials and their supporters has been most continuous and pronounced. This development intensified from the founding of the Fox News channel in 1996 onwards, and US conservatives have continually questioned the objectivity of the political coverage by independent or centrist news organizations ever since (Peck 2019). This challenge intensified with the rise of the Tea Party on the political right of establishment Republicans and has been epitomized by Sarah Palin's term "lamestream media" (Barr 2009). It reached a peak with Donald Trump's regular labelling of news organizations as "fake news," a label enthusiastically picked up by his supporters in contradicting coverage of their preferred candidates or positions. This aggressive delegitimation of news organizations has led to the emergence of a highly interconnected set of alternative news sites mainly on the far right, and digital media personalities who continually challenged the dominant media discourse and provided Trump supporters with alternative narratives and arguments. The longstanding attack on the legitimacy of independent news organizations continued with the contestation of the legitimacy of the Biden victory in the 2020 presidential election. The targeted erosion of the legitimacy of gatekeepers has thus presented a potential challenge to the legitimacy of US democracy itself (Przeworski 2019) and persists in an anti-state fringe within the US public arena.

Another challenge concerning the norms of journalistic coverage that emerged within American elite media and among journalism scholars is the idea of "moral clarity" toward the end of the Trump era (Gessen 2020; Lowery 2020). Moral clarity is essentially an argument that social justice should guide journalism, an idea that departs from the role of media as strictly impartial chroniclers and watchdogs. This argument opened a new fracture within the media and within the academy. As Jonathan Karl, a veteran White House reporter, put it toward the end of the Trump era: "We [the news media] are not the opposition party, but that is the way some of us acted, doing as much to undermine the credibility of the press as the president's taunts" (Karl 2020: xxv). This conflict has become apparent in the internal struggles among journalists working for the *New York Times* about the appropriate role for the paper (Wiedeman 2020).

The academy in the United States (and to a lesser extent in other Western democracies) has also been challenged regarding their autonomy and legitimacy as reliable sources of knowledge and information (Gauchat 2012; Rekker 2021). Instead of representing the impartial and exclusively evidence-driven institution of science, academics are in danger of being seen as going beyond their institutional role and pushing their own personal or partisan agendas. This, in turn, has given license to those who disagree with scientists to discard scientific and impartial knowledge, potentially endangering the legitimacy of academia itself (Levin 2020). The cost for academics of losing the legitimacy as impartial pursuers of fact can be vividly seen in the public discussion on climate change, with parts of the public rejecting scientific findings and advice depending on its perceived congruence or conflict with their political leaning (Hart & Nisbet 2012; Kahan *et al.* 2012).

While traditional institutions of the public arena face consistent challenges to their legitimacy, new infrastructures do so too. For some time, the journalistic and academic discussion of digital media have foregrounded their perceived risks for democracy and discourse. These challenges include claims of "echo chambers" or "filter bubbles" fragmenting discourse into homogenous groups, with people losing sight of political alternatives and thereby losing the ability to compromise (Sunstein 2017). Others have foregrounded the dangers of inauthentic or manipulative behaviour online, be it through (semi-)automated accounts – so-called bots – or users paid to interfere with democratic discourse (Kovic *et al.* 2018). More recently, commentators have focused on the perceived dangers of disinformation purposefully distributed via digital media (Bennett & Livingston 2021).

These and other claims have been given considerable purchase in traditional media, although their evidence base has been challenged. Various studies show that users of digital media tend not to cluster in politically homogenous groups and consistently get information well beyond their politically preferred camp (Flaxman *et al.* 2016; Scharkow *et al.* 2020; Webster 2014). Further, approaches routinely used to identify bots are notoriously unreliable (Rauchfleisch & Kaiser 2020a) and the activities of accounts reliably identified as bots do little to impact discourse on digital media (Keller *et al.* 2020), while disinformation online has far more limited reach than expected (Allen *et al.* 2020; Fletcher *et al.* 2018; Guess *et al.* 2020). The consistent prominence of stories that refer to these perceived dangers of digital media to democracy in public discourse and traditional media are thus not driven by the actual threat to democracy coming from these phenomena. Instead, they can be seen as part of an agenda whereby elites can challenge the legitimacy of digital media as emerging infrastructures of the public arena (Jungherr & Schroeder 2021).

The Chinese public arena is also alive with challenges to the legitimacy of participants. Centrally, public information about state failure and the corruption of public officials are a consistent threat to the legitimacy of the Chinese Communist Party and Chinese government. This has led to a pincer movement by the government of Xi Jinping: on the one hand, the party-state has cracked down on select cases of corruption while also keeping strict limits on what the Chinese press is allowed to cover. This challenge plays out most heavily on the local level of the Chinese state (Osnos 2014). At the same time, the digital public arena is also full of challenges, which include activists in support of increased freedom of speech. Or again, we find ultranationalists that publicly attack anyone critical of the Chinese government and nation while at the same time challenging the government for policies that are regarded as treasonous of Chinese interests abroad and insults to the Chinese national character. This ultranationalist challenge, also attacking progressive intellectual elites, thus in fact contributes to the stability of the party-state (Han 2018; Schroeder 2019).

   Against this backdrop of questioning the legitimacy of the public arena, we can also begin our suggestions for how to improve its role. We argue that the legitimacy of independent and fact-driven referees in the public arena is crucial going forward. We can already see that a journalism openly driven by "moral clarity" carries the risk of journalism jettisoning its position and its function as impartial referee of the public arena and of political competition. Thus supporters of different parties can, in their view legitimately, contest electoral outcomes, as seen during the 2020 US presidential election, with no common ground beyond partisan interest. A crisis of the public arena, result- ing in the contestation of shared rules and referees, thereby begins to erode the legitimacy of a whole political system and an anchor in evidence-based knowledge inasmuch as the body politic loses common ground without autonomous media and reliable knowledge. This bodes ill for the capacity of societies to react to unforeseen but transformative challenges such as climate change or pandemics.

5 Areas of Contention

These tensions of the public arena emerge at a time when it becomes obvious that even advanced societies face limits to the options available to them to react to societal challenges (Schroeder 2013). Advanced societies must address deep structural and external challenges, such as climate change and financial instabil- ity, combined with the threats of economic globalization. These are longstand- ing but intensifying tensions. To these established challenges can now be added the management and prevention of pandemics.

   Societies face threats that demand costly interventions that impose material constraints and limit personal freedoms. But these constraints are far from peoples' everyday experiences, as they are driven by the expectations and projections of experts and scientists concerned with extrapolating contemporary trends. They are thus far from evident or intuitive to the general public and even for many elite decision makers. This opens them up to contestation by interested parties (Oreskes & Conway 2010) or by people who might grasp the challenge but who are not yet ready to give up on an unsustainable lifestyle, especially in relation to risks expected in the future or in far-away places.

The acceptance of constraints and associated burdens based on expert testimonies and scientific evidence is therefore not a given. Instead, it depends on the acceptance of the credibility of experts and scientists, a belief in their competence, and trust that they have the best interest of the wider public at heart instead of serving their own interests or that of invested parties. This credibility is threatened by challenges from groups attacking the restraints imposed on them by politicians who at least in theory base their decisions on expert and scientific advice. These challenges not only focus on individual scientists, experts, or groups but also on the legitimacy of the scientific process and its epistemology as impartial arbiters of truth and facts. Accordingly, scientists and experts are treated as just another politically or culturally invested voice whose advice can be safely ignored. These conflicts are already starting to play out and offer a preview of the coming battle lines in the public arena.

Since early 2020, the world has been battling the COVID-19 pandemic. While the pandemic started out in the Chinese city of Wuhan, it quickly spread across the globe and demanded quick and strict interventions by governments and societies. Those societies able to organize a rapid and unified response, with people self-quarantining, wearing masks in public, or just in general reducing contacts with others, were successful in pushing the virus back quickly. Others, whose politicians wavered for political reasons, whose governments were too slow or unable to implement necessary interventions, or where the public splintered in support of necessary interventions or the severity of the risk, have been reduced to watching the virus spread through their populations.

Epidemiologists presented governments with models of expected virus spread and the likely consequences of interventions. They thus mapped the options available for governments to act and for politicians to present and negotiate alternatives. In the United States this was labelled by then president Donald Trump as an attempt to derail his re-election chances. Here, leading politicians and government officials not only rejected the advice of scientists and experts based on political motives but even negated the severity of the crisis. In Germany, on the other hand, the political system followed expert advice, for a long time uniformly, while opposition grew among a vocal and well-coordinated minority. In reaction to the government's interventions, there emerged a bottom-up grassroots movement that reached across the political left–right continuum, with far-right activists marching next to environmentalists. This minority used the opportunities provided by the new public arena to coordinate, create counter narratives, and share alternative media among the like-minded. They rejected the options left open to them by the narrowing of options through epidemiologists and health experts. Here, political contestation was not primarily driven by prior political allegiances but instead by deeply held personal values, distrust in capitalism, support of alternative lifestyle choices, and fears of increased state control. In China, meanwhile, the government has enjoyed increased legitimacy for its top-down efforts, although it did potentially endanger public health at the start of the pandemic due to the lack of an open and autonomous public arena that could have provided an early alert. In short, we can see the characteristics of the three public arenas clearly at work here.

The reactions to the pandemic are less important than what they presage for the future. Temporarily pushed off the top of the agenda of late, but still bound to feature prominently on the political, scientific, and economic agenda moving forward, is climate change. To avoid the expected runaway rise of temperatures in the near future, many governments have committed to lowering emissions of greenhouse gases to zero by 2050, which means reducing them significantly much earlier. Pragmatic roadmaps exist for the fulfilment of these goals. While many doubt the sincerity of these commitments – as shown in the widespread, international "Fridays for Future" climate protests in 2019 – agreement on these goals is a necessary first step to solving the underlying problem. The problem is diagnosed based on assessments, models, and prognoses by experts and scientists. But while there is widespread agreement on the general trend (temperatures rising on average) and its causes (human-made) among experts and scientists, it is far from clear that their science-based consensus will enjoy continued legitimacy or garner sufficient awareness in a crowded attention space. In fact, experts and scientists recommend interventions that significantly impact the economy of nations and the welfare and freedom of individuals based on the authority of scientific institutions that must be accepted on trust by non-scientists. The mechanics of the models underlying the prognoses, the long time horizons involved, and the effects of a seemingly harmless average temperature increase of 1.5 to 2 degrees make it hard for members of the public to intuitively grasp the underlying reasoning. Acceptance of climate change scenarios and support of interventions aimed at stopping them thus depends on trust in experts and scientists, their epistemologies, and their disinterestedness.

Even the most pragmatic approaches to dealing with climate change demand significant and far-reaching interventions by states and limit the actions and degrees of freedom of businesses and individuals. Pursuing these goals means shutting down industries, such as coal, and deeply transforming others, such as agriculture and steel and cement production. Even the most pragmatic roadmaps expect a rise in energy prices, impacting consumers and the competitiveness of heavily energy-dependent industries, risking further unemployment. They also demand the development and widespread implementation of new energy sources, often perceived by citizens as a nuisance or health threat, such as local wind farms. The goal of collectively reducing emissions can extend as far as telling people how to build houses, what to eat, or what type of clothes to wear. This is bound to lead to political contestation and will demand skilled political leadership. Climate activists see public reactions to the COVID-19 pandemic as an example of the kinds of interventions that are possible if governments take a crisis seriously and choose to act. This is bound to increase the pressure they try to exert on governments. Beyond activism, we can already see in the United States the costs of allowing climate policy to devolve into a contentious political issue in the public arena, with the Democrats accepting the prospect of man-made climate change and the Republicans widely disputing the scientific diagnoses. This shows the lack of society-wide acceptance of the limited options urged by experts and scientists.

Intersecting with these two crises are the constraints imposed on governments and publics by economic globalization. International integration reduces degrees of freedom for countries and their populace in their democratic decision making (Rodrik 2011). International treaties, such as those for international trade, are widely contested as limiting the autonomy for democratic decision making and are a source of broad public opposition in Western democracies (Jungherr *et al.* 2018). Similarly, the global financial and debt crisis of 2008 illustrated the instability of the financial system and with it the limits of the fiscal autonomy of nation states (Schroeder 2013). This degree of international connection has been weaponized as mutual dependency (Drezner *et al.* 2021; Farrell & Newman 2019b) and strategically used by states. Suffice it to say that these dependencies follow legal, economic, and scientific epistemologies and not the sways of public opinion at large. Accordingly, this is another area where experts and scientists can come into conflict with public opinion.

These cases show three domains in which different groups of scientists and experts (i.e. epidemiologists, climate scientists, and economists) analyze problems, run models, form prognoses, and present them to politicians and a wider public. In all three cases, there is a consensus among scientists and experts – who are practitioners of the same epistemology and rely on evidence – which in turn is relied upon but also contested by politicians, interest groups, and citizens. These contestations usually do not follow the same epistemic rules and evidence base that experts and scientists followed in providing advice. Instead, they represent contestations of the legitimacy of the advice and rejections of the appropriateness of reliable knowledge and data for a given question. For example, the issue is not about how to model the spread of a virus but how to account for the human costs of isolation and economic hardship. The issue is not about rising temperatures but how to cushion the expected economic blows for those employed in heavily impacted sectors of the economy. The issue is not whether economic models indicate the need for austerity policies, but if these models account for enough of human life or the boundaries of economic protection as to be meaningful.

The opposition to experts is already a common feature among populist challengers and other civil society challengers but it could spread more widely if these crises further increase reliance on expertise that constrain political options, and media and professional institutions weaken. This opposition questions the legitimacy of experts and scientists to limit the will of the people.

Once peoples' options in exercising their occupations or personal freedoms become narrowed by the say-so of experts and scientists, people will challenge their legitimacy. This might not be true for a majority (Bertsou & Caramani 2020), especially since the COVID-19 pandemic seems to have led to an increase in popular trust in scientists. A heavily mobilized, highly interconnected critical minority might be enough, however, to mount an effective challenge. One early example is the "Querdenker" (contrarian thinkers) movement in Germany, a vocal and increasingly radicalized minority in Germany opposed to the government's interventions to stop the spread of COVID-19, which attacks leading epidemiologists and sees scientists as being in the pocket of Big Pharma. When scientific epistemologies and expert advice increasingly set the agenda in a consensus-oriented public arena, their position in difficult times is bound to be challenged. This atmosphere threatens to unearth the inherent potential conflict that emerges between science and democracy when an objective approach to understand and explain the world comes to be seen as a "religion of an elite" (Lippman 1928: 39) – in this case a technocratic elite – and accordingly democratically rejected.

The structural tensions of public arenas described above force these conflicts into the open. Just as politicians and journalists before them (Gurri 2018), scientists and experts can find their institutional standing or authority challenged (Levin 2020) and must face their challengers in the public arena and defend their epistemologies and conclusions. This is vital and justified if they expect for their advice to limit the opportunities, choices, economic prospects, and personal freedoms if followed by governments.[3] Western democratic institutions especially may have to get used to the noise and heat of the contemporary public arena instead of hoping to somehow turn back the clock to a centralized and orderly public arena.

---

[3] This means also stepping away from fashionable relativistic posturing. It is notable here that even academics in the field of science and technology studies, whose main stance has been to deny the objectivity of science for several decades, now, in the face of climate change and the pandemic,

6 The Public Arena: Conditions, Consequences, and Responsibilities

As we have seen, contemporary societies face tensions that are negotiated in public arenas. At the same time, digital technology has led to structural transformations of these public arenas that are yet ill understood and not analyzed systematically. Recent challenges, such as pandemics, climate change, and economic globalization add to these. Instead of addressing these tensions and working toward pragmatic solutions, elites have been focused on blaming digital technology. Thus, much intellectual energy and collective attention has been ill spent and we are little further in developing or pursuing constructive alternatives.

We have defined the public arena as the media infrastructures that enable and constrain the publication, distribution, reception, and contestation of information allowing people to exercise their rights and duties as citizens. These infrastructures mediate the relation between citizens or civil society on the one hand and political elites or the state on the other. The make-up, governance, and use of media infrastructures are central to society's pursuit of the public good.

Like McQuail (2013: 202) we argue that the public arena must provide "diverse and reliable information" and ensure "effective self-government." There remains a tension between media infrastructures providing a minimum of cohesion in society while also providing information on diverse viewpoints that challenge the societal status quo. These ideas need to be expanded in view of the extensions of the public arena to include new digital infrastructures – such as search engines or digital platforms – that provide important additions to it. Given their importance to the public arena, these infrastructures need to accept demands for governance oversight and being transparent to regulators and the public about their contribution to the public arena and their related internal governance rules and processes (Kaye 2019; Napoli 2019). While they do not share the burdens and privileges of journalism in covering politics and society, they must still ensure, in their role as gateways to information and spaces for people to get their voice heard, that they do not harm, but instead enhance, public discourse.

---

admit the error of their ways and are switching course. For example, Bruno Latour now says: "We will have to regain some of the authority of science. That is the complete opposite from where we started doing science studies" (de Vrieze 2017: 159). Harry Collins and colleagues now say "science and technology studies ... unwittingly supports the rise of populism ... it should no longer simply celebrate the erosion of sciences [sic] cultural preeminence" (Collins *et al.* 2020: 1).

First, the public arena of many nations now includes media infrastructures that started out by providing services to people in private or commercial contexts. Companies providing these media infrastructures must recognize their role in shaping the public arena in many countries and accept their corresponding responsibilities. This means transparently developing and documenting their adherence to governance rules in the service of an articulated and contestable normative concept of the public arena and their contribution to it. Ideally, companies are not left to develop idiosyncratic and necessarily self-serving governance rules on their own but will instead do so in conjunction with national governments and international institutions, in the contexts of existing international or national laws and regulation.

Second, media infrastructures are bound by local laws and regulations in the countries they operate in. For companies providing media infrastructures that contribute to the public arenas of many different countries, this presents a challenge. While Western democracies guarantee, perhaps imperfectly, universal rights of freedom of opinion and expression guaranteed in Article 19 of the Universal Declaration of Human Rights, many non- or transitional democracies in practice do not. Adhering to respective local laws and regulations may lead companies to allow their infrastructures to be used by governments for the repression of opinions and expression and even the persecution of political opponents. This is untenable. Companies should commit themselves to an internationally recognized consensus on freedom of opinion and expression and respective regulation. In countries where governments try to force them to deviate from this, they need to make these requests public and if need be accept being banned in these respective territories. Over time, this will mean that different country blocs use different media structures to constitute their public arenas and conform to locally accepted governance rules regarding freedom of opinion and expression. While this might feel like a regression, given the ambitious goals of the borderless Internet emerging from the California of the 1980s and 1990s, it is a necessary consequence of international variance regarding the legitimate governance of the public arena and individual rights and the international importance of digital infrastructures in the national negotiation of the public good. Accordingly, the international reach of companies providing digital infrastructure will extend to the same degree as geopolitical competition between countries and associated blocs weakens and contract as competition strengthens. Accordingly, the limits of their reach will map the borders of said competition.

This also has consequences for the academic comparison of different media systems. While the approach introduced by Hallin and Mancini (2004), focusing on political, regulatory, and historical contexts of media systems, proved to be a powerful framework, for the contemporary public arena, we need to account for at least two further factors. The first of these is the country of origin for dominant digital media infrastructures in a country's public arena. Here, we are likely to find significant differences with regard to the degree of state control for infrastructures provided by companies based in the United States or China. The second factor is the regulatory tradition of rights to privacy and political speech, which will play an important role in the governance of digital infrastructures. Here, we currently see the greatest difference between the legal traditions in the United States and the EU, leading to different governance approaches for digital infrastructures, even if they are provided by US-based companies.

Third, media infrastructures provide the staging area of political competition and societal contestation. In this regard, they are not neutral. Specific constellations of media infrastructures favor specific societal actors. For example, a set of diverse and decentralized infrastructures supports the challenge of established institutions and control, while a small set of centrally controlled infrastructures tend to strengthen the position of established institutions and control (Castells 2013). In the contemporary public arena, we find both constellations. On the one hand, digital media allow for the emergence of many new sources of information, while on the other the growing influence of digital platforms on the shaping of public attention centralizes control. The current temptation is to use these central structures to shape political competition and to deny unruly voices and factions access. This is problematic. While media infrastructures must control content regarding whether it is legal, harmful, or violates rights, this brings many challenges regarding political speech. While speech needs to be moderated, it is also clear that societies should not outsource the duty to adjudicate political conflict to media infrastructures. Otherwise, media infrastructures will lose legitimacy qua providers of reliable and diverse but also open information and their contribution to the public arena will splinter into providing access to select factions. This will undoubtedly sharpen political conflict and reduce the ability for societal compromise while at the same time hiding the grievances, the strengths of different views, and allegiance to legitimate or illegitimate challenges to the societal status quo.

Fourth, norms of discourse are changing. Personal threats or group-based attacks on elites, public figures, or participants in online conversations are not acceptable. Infrastructure providers need to offer transparent, easy-to-use, and direct approaches for the deletion and potential bans of those who originate attacks and threats. Still, this is likely to be after the fact so the harm to targeted individuals will already be done. Also, politicians may try to use these standards of unacceptable behaviour to squelch legitimate criticism. Therefore, unruly and hostile contributions to the public arena will remain a significant structural challenge for platforms and those affected. While moderation can address some of these concerns, the only tenable interim solution is a shift in discursive norms toward more civil and constructive contributions. Still, public criticism, challenges, and unruliness are necessarily baked into the structure of the extended public arena and some degree of deviance will be inevitable.

Fifth, the mutual tethering of different sources in the public arena has mixed effects. On the one hand, tethering central news organizations to digital extensions of the public arena can contribute to the diversity of the voices, factions, and groups represented in public discourse. This is positive. On the other, some of these voices, factions, and groups – such as extremists on either end of the political spectrum that aim to restrict the rights of others – have been excluded from the public arena for good reason. Seeing these groups using digital media to share information, coordinate and radicalize supporters, and force their way into the center of political discourse is troubling. Beyond this, digital media do not offer a balanced view of public opinion in terms of priorities or the population at large. Hence they can be biased sources of political interests and views (Jungherr *et al.* 2016, 2017). They are decidedly not cheap alternatives to opinion surveys, although they are sometimes used in this way. This calls for efforts to identify skews in digitally manifested public views, digitally enabled misrepresentation of public opnion, and a weighing of the benefits and dangers of this closer mutual tethering.

Citizens also need to accept greater responsibility for their informational behavior in the public arena. They need to choose not only media and political options that fit their own narrow interests or inclinations but instead seek out those that provide common benefits and better equip them to fulfil their responsibilities as citizens. Treating the quality of democratic discourse as merely a supply-side problem and focusing on providers of information and infrastructures ignores the demand-side problem with many people checking out of politics or treating it as an entertaining blood sport. Not taking advantage of diverse online offerings but also choosing those that challenge one's views or enrich one's perspectives and evidence for sound judgment comes with costs. This also raises the demands for education systems in their development of responsible citizens equipped to deal with and confront political conflict in the expanded public arena – in other words, fostering engaged citizenship.

Finally, the extended set of media infrastructures in the public arena make it increasingly difficult to assess its structures, interdependencies, and effects. Here, the companies running media infrastructures new and old need to work more actively with lawmakers, civil society, and researchers to surface, understand, and address potential threats.

Beyond these general observations, there are specific take-aways from our cases regarding two themes: how the public arena provides space for challenges to the status quo and the role of the public arena as staging ground for societal conflict.

Challenges to the Status Quo

In China, the expanded public arena remains managed. But even here the authorities need to cope with new voices and backlash generated within certain areas in this expanded public arena: the government should embrace them. In Germany, the challengers who have taken advantage of this added scope of the public arena find their reach limited by public service media, the established parties, and government. But the expanded parts of the public arena give space to those dissatisfied with various aspects of the status quo, provide them with opportunities to form broad alliances of the dissatisfied, and offer opportunities for challenger parties to emerge that take this dissatisfaction from the fringes of public attention into the center, making it more fractious. This means that their challenge to the status quo – such as their criticism of public broadcasting and large commercial newspapers – needs to be answered and shown to be misplaced. In other words, their dissatisfaction with the status quo needs to be channeled into constructive political competition where justified, and publicly contested where unjustified. In the United States, the added scope of the public arena has amplified the centripetal forces of elite plural politics and of civil society. While diverse groups with diverse agendas, interests, and grievances find themselves torn by advancing multiple non-overlapping agendas in the public arena, they nevertheless must meld with either of the two parties, themselves straining since they must compete for a center where majoritarian success has become elusive. This produces intensified political gridlock since the diverse group interests cannot be incorporated in a common agenda of either party, thereby internalizing struggles between the center and fractious forces within the parties, instead of opening this struggle to electoral competition in a system with compromises among interests that are perceived as partly overlapping: such compromises will be sorely needed in shaping a nationally cohesive agenda that seeks to regain a leading role among nations.

Currently, there is a risk of characterizing the digital extension to the public arena as inherently unruly, hostile, manipulative, and discriminatory. While there are clear excesses in the way politics is discussed and negotiated in digital media that need to be addressed, an overemphasis on these aspects allows forces of the status quo to delegitimize any challenge that forms in digital media without having to engage it on the merits of the arguments. While this might be an easy choice at a time when digital challenges wear the mask of populist far-right politics, it is worth remembering that the next progressive movement or democratic enlargement toward a more diverse and inclusive politics may depend on online challengers, their audiences, or supporters – as was the case with Bernie Sanders or the Pirate Party – or on ideas that are currently fermenting in hidden or less visible online spaces. Establishing precedents of over-regulating unruly speech and challenges when one deems a challenge of the societal status quo unjustified may hinder subsequent legitimate and necessary challenges availing themselves of the same opportunities. The same goes for the rules of political speech in non-Western democracies or autocracies. The rules for digital infrastructure must work in Western democracies, authoritarian regimes, and beyond. Pulling the reigns tight on dissent in Western democracies will weaken challenges in other contexts.

In general, the search for solutions to contemporary crises should focus more on providing substantive alternatives aimed at solving common challenges or addressing deep structural tensions, rather than on the moderation or tone by which political challenges are expressed. Here, alternative agendas expressed via digital and other media can offer interesting perspectives and should not be discarded outright, except if they only provide destructive contributions to public discourse or attack its representatives. Apart from tackling online harms, search engines and social media companies can do much to contribute to a healthier overall media environment. So can citizens and civil society when they reward contributors, sources, and infrastructures with their attention or punish them by shifting attention to others. And likewise political elites, who can force the providers of instructures to take seriously their responsibilities as hosts of the public arena by introducing and enforcing regulation and obligations for increased transparency.

There are more specific constructive ideas arising from our analysis in the three cases. For China, we are persuaded by Slater and Wang's proposition of democratizing from a position of strength: the party-elite leadership can play a role in encouraging pluralism and democracy while it still has the possibility to do so without its legitimacy reaching a crisis point. In other words, there are options for the party-elite to take constructive steps and not just rely on an imposed segmentation of its critics which blocks the more profound changes needed toward a democratic order and more autonomous public arena (Slater & Wong 2013). In the United States, governments and parties need to develop policies and party programs of more universal – broader and deeper – citizenship. Restricting citizenship for political – majoritarian – gain goes against the American creed of opportunities for all; though there are trade-offs in how this creed can be implemented (Schroeder 2020). But these trade-offs, such as around open economic borders, need to be subject to constructive democratic inputs. For Germany, fractious fringes need to decide whether to remain side-shows of the disaffected or to contribute to addressing the actual drivers of unrepresented grievances. For this they need to shed their exclusivist, anti-modernist, and anti-science elements. Only this will allow them to channel the interests of fractious fringes into productive directions while leaving merely negative obstructionist and discriminatory ones out in the cold.

Conflicts

The public arena is a space of structured and mediated conflict. Conflict as such is therefore not a sign of the pathology of the public arena but instead its natural expression. By enabling and making broadly visible challenges to the status quo, digital media produce frictions within and between countries and macro-regions. Currently, this takes the form of challenges to political authority that seek more cultural autonomy within and that contest the transnationalizing order externally. But this cultural challenge takes different forms: against an open economy (increasingly in the United States and partly also in China), against open borders (based more on economic motives in the Unites States, and more on political motives in Germany and Europe), and against an open culture in China. Further, there are specific challenges, against open and reliable knowledge, though not in China, where politics is not open to knowledge contestation in the first place.

All these challenges compete for recognition in a limited media space. The ensuing conflicts find their strongest expression in the digital extension of the public arena. Only a comprehensive account of media allows us to weigh these challenges and identify gaps in theory and evidence, but also go forward to suggest measures to improve the mediated public arena.

First, instead of diagnosing the root cause of conflict as manipulation and misinformation in the public arena, we need to recognize that the public arena is naturally contested as a conduit between states and civil societies. To allow for this contest to play out effectively, infrastructures of the public arena need to keep or regain broad acceptance as impartial, inclusive, diverse, and objective conduits for information that allow people to exercise their rights and duties as citizens. By impartiality we mean representing the interests and views of civil society and the state in as comprehensive or inclusive, diverse or pluralistic, and objective or impartial way as possible. This includes exercising a watchdog function where needed. Importantly, this goes beyond providing a balanced forum for views held by parties represented in parliament (Wahl-Jorgensen *et al.* 2017). It includes featuring views held in civil society and by citizens even if not represented by party democracy at that time. At the same time, this does not mean simply giving equal time and weight to every view or every argument. Instead, news organizations in the public arena need to weigh positions and views based on their relevance for society at large or their factualness. This process will be contested and news organizations will struggle with this. But this contestation and this public struggle are an important part of the negotiation of the agenda in the public arena and therefore cannot be avoided.

Search engines and social media do not have this function of news organizations, but they also must not distort political competition and instead have the responsibility to add to the benefits of digital infrastructures. Accordingly, the digital extension of the public arena also needs to be open, including the option to contest traditional media and the political status quo, and regulated only when clearly harmful. Apart from ruling out certain types of harmful content – especially content harassing individuals or groups – the new characteristics and patterns of gatekeeping in these extended areas and infrastructures need to be deepened and broadened. This includes not just openness, but also diversity and inclusiveness and helping to strengthen the impartiality, objectivity, and the watchdog function of the public arena. Therefore, the digital extensions of the public arena need to become more managed and orderly, but only in the manner of inoculating against harm rather than imposing a new arbiter to political conflicts. This will make them a more useful and reliable part of the public arena. Traditional media and news must stay above the social media fray, not get pulled in by the skewed audience-drivenness of social media.

It is futile to hope for the re-emergence of central and monopolistic gatekeepers that will stop political conflict or at least push it out of sight. At the heart of this wish lies a view of human society that sees political and social conflict as an information problem: if all people could just have the same high-quality information, the body politic would agree on the best way forward. But this might focus on the wrong issue. In times of multiple tensions, it is easy to forget the benefits of noisy and unruly public arenas and that most users of digital media are neither extremists nor actively interested in politics for that matter. While malicious uses of digital media are real and must be countered vigilantly, they are far from the main story. Solutions involving government control of the public arena should address the tensions that digital transformations have surfaced instead of trying to suppress them.

At present, the pendulum swings clearly to the side of providing more controls in the public arena. Yet we should not let suggestive stories of deviance or of the momentary successes of extremists allow us to lose sight of the contribution of open debate and exchange of alternatives. Detrimental effects of the expanded public arena need to be identified, empirically measured, and dealt with. But the same goes for the much less tangible but equally real benefits that an expanded public arena has brought to political discourse and collective problem-solving worldwide. The challenges the world currently faces are too big to think that they can be addressed without the noisy and sometimes unruly expanded digital public arena.

7 Coda

It is easy to see how widespread insecurities and distrust in the infrastructures of the public arena have emerged. The widely observed but ill-chronicled and ill-understood shifts in the public arena raise legitimate questions about how the contemporary public arena functions and who benefits from this in societal and political competition. In the past these questions were addressed by shared norms among journalists that made "the press" into a social institution. Journalism shared a code of impartial coverage, clearly identified areas of commentary, and pursued standards of quality control in content production. These shared norms were widely discussed and recognized in society so that political elites and the public knew what to expect from journalism and were equipped to challenge it if they felt that journalists or the medium transgressed or fell short. Of course, these standards and norms were far from universally adhered to and sometimes contested, but that was not their point. By providing a clear guidepost by which to measure specific behavior or content, journalism could be evaluated and legitimately contested.

These guideposts seem to be missing in the contemporary public arena. For the discussion to evolve and to move toward a better equilibrium, a broad discussion about the norms and governance for the newly structured public arena is needed. This will make the underlying norms and boundaries explicit and reign in the hysteria associated with much of the discussion about the digital extension to the public arena. These new structures are here to stay, so we need to focus our thinking on how the public arena and its extensions can revitalize public discourse: these extensions can bolster the vibrancy of civil society and provide more reliable and diverse information available to citizens, if audience-drivenness is supplemented by more transparent workings and greater efforts to enhance the diversity and reliability of information.

More generally, there are implications of our argument for scholarship, in particular for working across different disciplines in the analysis of structural changes in the public arena. For example, communication science is highly attuned to the changes in media, content, and user behavior – but often neglects the embeddedness of communication in larger social structures. This has led scholars to overestimate the importance of the phenomenon of communication. Sociology and political science are deeply attuned to the structures of social life, but they neglect – or in any case have few tools to analyze – the role of media and communication. We have combined the two and presented an argument that puts both communications and its structural constraints and transformations into comparative perspective, thereby illustrating the complementary strengths of both research traditions.

With this Element, we have argued that systematic comparison and analysis of the whole media landscape is essential, but also that the analysis of the public arena must include how it mediates between elites and civil society. Remedies to current challenges and tensions that focus exclusively on media or digital media are therefore only one part of the solution and must be put in the context of how they chime with the possibilities and constraints of different settings, including the media systems and the geopolitics of macro-regions of where digital infrastructures are located and compete. Further, the autonomy of media institutions and their professional norms, as well as the role of expert elites, but also the responsibilities of political leaders and citizens, must play their part. This is a complicated picture, but a structural account of the public arena deserves no less.

References

Agarwal, S. D., and Barthel, M. L. (2015). The Friendly Barbarians: Professional Norms and Work Routines of Online Journalists in the United States. *Journalism*, **16**(3), 376–91.

Allen, J., Howland, B., Mobius, M., Rothschild, D., and Watts, D. J. (2020). Evaluating the Fake News Problem at the Scale of the Information Ecosystem. *Science Advances*, **6**(14), eaay3539.

Barr, A. (2009). Palin Trashes "Lamestream Media". *Politco*. www .politico.com/story/2009/11/palin-trashes-lamestream-media-029693.

Bennett, W. L., and Livingston, S., eds. (2021). *The Disinformation Age: Politics, Technology, and Disruptive Communication in the United States*. Cambridge: Cambridge University Press. DOI: https://doi.org/10.1017 /9781108914628.

Bensmann, M., Eckert, T., and Richter, F. (2020). "Hygiene-Demos": Russland-Freunde gegen Corona. *Correctiv*. https://correctiv.org/aktuelles/2020/04/30/ hygiene-demos-russland-freunde-gegen-corona.

Bertsou, E., and Caramani, D. (2020). People Haven't Had Enough of Experts: Technocratic Attitudes among European Citizens. *American Journal of Political Science*. DOI: https://doi.org/10.1111/ajps.12554.

Bieber, C., and Leggewie, C., eds. (2012). *Unter Piraten: Erkundungen in einer neuen politischen Arena*. Bielefeld: Transcript.

Bimber, B. (2003). *Information and American Democracy: Technology in the Evolution of Political Power*. Cambridge: Cambridge University Press.

Blum, R. M. (2020). *How the Tea Party Captured the GOP: Insurgent Factions in American Politics*. Champaign, IL: University of Chicago Press.

Bond, P. (2016). Leslie Moonves on Donald Trump: "It May Not Be Good for America, but It's Damn Good for CBS." *The Hollywood Reporter*. www.hollywoodreporter.com/news/leslie-moonves-donald-trump-may -871464.

Bonikowski, B. (2019). Trump's Populism: The Mobilization of Nationalist Cleavages and the Future of US Democracy. In K. Weyland and R. L. Madrid, eds. *When Democracy Trumps Populism: European and Latin American Lessons for the United States*. Cambridge: Cambridge University Press, 110–31.

Bradford, A. (2020). *The Brussels Effect: How the European Union Rules the World*. Oxford: Oxford University Press.

Campbell, J. L. (2018). *American Discontent: The Rise of Donald Trump*, New York: Oxford University Press.

Castells, M. (2013). *Communication Power*, 2nd ed. Oxford: Oxford University Press.

Claggett, W. J. M., Engle, P. J., and Shafer, B. E. (2014). The Evolution of Mass Ideologies in Modern American Politics. *The Forum*, **12**(2), 223–56.

Cohen, M., Karol, D., Noel, H., and Zaller, J. (2008). *The Party Decides: Presidential Nominations before and after Reform*. Chicago, IL: University of Chicago Press.

Collins, H., Evans, R., Durant, D., and Weinel, M. (2020). *Experts and the Will of the People: Society, Populism and Science*. Basingstoke: Palgrave Macmillan.

Collins, R. (2021). Assault on the Capitol: 2021, 1917, 1792. *The Sociological Eye: Writings by the Sociologist Randall Collins*. http://sociological-eye.blogspot.com/2021/01/assault-on-capitol-2021-1917-1792.html.

Cramer, K. J. (2016). *Politics of Resentment: Rural Consciousness in Wisconsin and the Rise of Scott Walker*. Chicago, IL: University of Chicago Press.

de Vrieze, J. (2017). "Science Wars" Veteran Has a New Mission. *Science*, **358** (6360), 159.

Der Spiegel Staff (2019). Documents Link AfD Parliamentarian to Moscow. *Der Spiegel*. www.spiegel.de/international/germany/documents-link-afd-parliamentarian-to-moscow-a-1261509.html.

Diakopoulos, N. (2019). *Automating the News: How Algorithms Are Rewriting the Media*. Cambridge, MA: Harvard University Press.

Douek, E. (2019). Facebook's "Oversight Board": Move Fast with Stable Infrastructure and Humility. *North Carolina Journal of Law and Technology*, **21**(1), 1–78.

Douek, E. (2021). Governing Online Speech: From "Posts-as-Trumps" to Proportionality and Probability. *Columbia Law Review*, **121**(3), 759–834.

Drezner, D. W., Farrell, H., and Newman, A. L., eds. (2021). *The Uses and Abuses of Weaponized Interdependence*. Washington, DC: Brookings Institution Press.

Drüeke, R., and Zobl, E. (2016). Online Feminist Protest against Sexism: The German-language Hashtag #aufschrei. *Feminist Media Studies*, **16**(1), 35–54.

Dubois, E., and Blank, G. (2018). The Echo Chamber is Overstated: The Moderating Effect of Political Interest and Diverse Media. *Information, Communication & Society*, **21**(5), 729–45.

Duina, F. (2018). *Broke and Patriotic: Why Poor Americans Love Their Country*. Stanford, CA: Stanford University Press.

Eimeren, B. van, Simon, E., and Riedl, A. (2017). Medienvertrauen und Informationsverhalten von politischen Zweiflern und Entfremdeten. *Media Perspektiven*, (11), 538–54.

Eldridge, S. A. (2018). *Online Journalism from the Periphery: Interloper Media and the Journalistic Field*. London: Routledge. DOI: https://doi.org/10.4324 /9781315671413.

Emirbayer, M., and Desmond, M. (2015). *The Racial Order*. Chicago, IL: University of Chicago Press.

Erie, M. S., and Streinz, T. (2021). The Beijing Effect: China's Digital Silk Road as Transnational Data Governance. *Social Science Research Network*. https://ssrn.com/abstract=3810256.

Farrell, H., and Newman, A. L. (2019a). *Of Privacy and Power: The Transatlantic Struggle over Freedom and Security*. Princeton, NJ: Princeton University Press.

Farrell, H., and Newman, A. L. (2019b). Weaponized Interdependence: How Global Economic Networks Shape State Coercion. *International Security*, **44** (1), 42–79.

Fiorina, M. P. (2017). *Unstable Majorities: Polarization, Party Sorting, and Political Stalemate*. Stanford, CA: Hoover Institution Press.

Flaxman, S., Goel, S., and Rao, J. M. (2016). Filter Bubbles, Echo Chambers, and Online News Consumption. *Public Opinion Quarterly*, **80**(1), 298–320.

Fletcher, R., Cornia, A., Graves, L., and Nielsen, R. K. (2018). *Measuring the Reach of "Fake News" and Online Disinformation in Europe*. Reuters Institute for the Study of Journalism. https://reutersinstitute.politics .ox.ac.uk/sites/default/files/2018-02/Measuring.

Fraser, N. (1990). Rethinking the Public Sphere: A Contribution to the Critique of Actually Existing Democracy. *Social Text*, (25/26), 56–80.

Freelon, D., Marwick, A., and Kreiss, D. (2020). False Equivalencies: Online Activism from Left to Right. *Science*, **369**(6508), 1197–201.

Fukuyama, F., and Grotto, A. (2020). Comparative Media Regulation in the United States and Europe. In N. Persily and J. A. Tucker, eds. *Social Media and Democracy: The State of the Field, Prospects for Reform*. Cambridge: Cambridge University Press, 199–219.

Gäbler, B. (2018). *AfD und Medien: Erfahrungen und Lehren für die Praxis*. Frankfurt am Main: Otto Brenner Stiftung.

Gatehouse, G. (2017). Marine le Pen: Who's Funding France's Far Right? *BBC News*. www.bbc.com/news/world-europe-39478066.

Gauchat, G. (2012). Politicization of Science in the Public Sphere: A Study of Public Trust in the United States, 1974 to 2010. *American Sociological Review*, **77**(2), 167–87.

Gessen, M. (2020). Why Are Some Journalists Afraid of "Moral Clarity"? *The New Yorker*. www.newyorker.com/news/our-columnists/why-are-some-journalists-afraid-of-moral-clarity.

Gilardi, F., Gessler, T., Kubli, M., and Müller, S. (2021). Social Media and Political Agenda Setting. *Political Communication*. DOI: https://doi.org/10.1080/10584609.2021.1910390.

Gorski, P. S. (2020). *American Babylon: Christianity and Democracy before and after Trump*. Abingdon: Routledge.

Gorwa, R. (2019). What Is Platform Governance? *Information, Communication & Society*, **22**(6), 854–71.

Gorwa, R. (2021). Elections, Institutions, and the Regulatory Politics of Platform Governance: The Case of the German NetzDG. *Telecommunications Policy*, **45**(6), 102145.

Gorwa, R., Binns, R., and Katzenbach, C. (2020). Algorithmic Content Moderation: Technical and Political Challenges in the Automation of Platform Governance. *Big Data & Society*, **7**(1), 1–15.

Guess, A. M., Nyhan, B., and Reifler, J. (2020). Exposure to Untrustworthy Websites in the 2016 US Election. *Nature Human Behavior*, **4**, 472–80.

Guhl, J., Ebner, J., and Rau, J. (2020). *The Online Ecosystem of the German Far-Right*. London: Institute for Strategic Dialogue (ISD). www.isdglobal.org/wp-content/uploads/2020/02/ISD-The-Online-Ecosystem-of-the-German-Far-Right-English-Draft-11.pdf.

Guhl, J., and Gerster, L. (2020). *Crisis and Loss of Control: German-Language Digital Extremism in the Context of the COVID-19 Pandemic*. London: Institute for Strategic Dialogue (ISD). www.isdglobal.org/isd-publications/crisis-and-loss-of-control-german-language-digital-extremism-in-the-context-of-the-covid-19-pandemic.

Gurri, M. (2018). *The Revolt of the Public and the Crisis of Authority in the New Millennium*, 2nd ed. San Francisco, CA: Stripe Press.

Habermas, J. (1962). *Strukturwandel der Öffentlichkeit: Untersuchungen zu einer Kategorie der bürgerlichen Gesellschaft*. Neuwied: Hermann Luchterhand Verlag.

Hall, J. A., and Lindholm, C. (1999). *Is America Breaking Apart?* Princeton, NJ: Princeton University Press.

Haller, A., and Holt, K. (2019). Paradoxical Populism: How PEGIDA Relates to Mainstream and Alternative Media. *Information, Communication & Society*, **22**(12), 1665–80.

Haller, M. (2017). *Die "Flüchtlingskrise" in den Medien*. Frankfurt am Main: Otto Brenner Stiftung.

Hallin, D. C., and Mancini, P. (2004). *Comparing Media Systems: Three Models of Media and Politics*. Cambridge: Cambridge University Press.

Han, R. (2018). *Contesting Cyberspace in China: Online Expression and Authoritarian Resilience*. New York: Columbia University Press.

Harder, R. A., Sevenans, J., and Van Aelst, P. (2017). Intermedia Agenda Setting in the Social Media Age: How Traditional Players Dominate the News Agenda in Election Times. *The International Journal of Press/ Politics*, **22**(3), 275–93.

Hart, P. S., and Nisbet, E. C. (2012). Boomerang Effects in Science Communication: How Motivated Reasoning and Identity Cues Amplify Opinion Polarization about Climate Mitigation Policies. *Communication Research*, **39**(6), 701–23.

Heft, A., Knüpfer, C., Reinhardt, S., and Mayerhöffer, E. (2021). Toward a Transnational Information Ecology on the Right? Hyperlink Networking among Right-Wing Digital News Sites in Europe and the United States. *The International Journal of Press/Politics*, **26**(2), 484–504.

Heilmann, S. (2008). From Local Experiments to National Policy: The Origins of China's Distinctive Policy Process. *The China Journal*, **59**, 1–30.

Herbst, S. (1993). *Numbered Voices: How Opinion Polling Has Shaped American Politics*. Chicago, IL: University of Chicago Press.

Huang, H. (2017). A War of (Mis)Information: The Political Effects of Rumors and Rumor Rebuttals in an Authoritarian Country. *British Journal of Political Science*, **47**(2), 283–311.

Hughes, T. P. (1983). *Networks of Power: Electrification in Western Society, 1880–1930*. Baltimore, MD: Johns Hopkins University Press.

Igo, S. (2007). *The Averaged American: Surveys, Citizens, and the Making of a Mass Public*. Cambridge, MA: Harvard University Press.

Jackson, S. J., Bailey, M., and Welles, B. F. (2020). *#HashtagActivism: Networks of Race and Gender Justice*. Cambridge, MA: The MIT Press.

Jardina, A. (2019). *White Identity Politics*. Cambridge: Cambridge University Press.

Josephson, P. R. (2005). *Resources under Regimes: Technology, Environment, and the State*. Cambridge, MA: Harvard University Press.

Jungherr, A. (2014). The Logic of Political Coverage on Twitter: Temporal Dynamics and Content. *Journal of Communication*, **64**(2), 239–59.

Jungherr, A., and Jürgens, P. (2014). Through a Glass, Darkly: Tactical Support and Symbolic Association in Twitter Messages Commenting on Stuttgart 21. *Social Science Computer Review*, **32**(1), 74–89.

Jungherr, A., Mader, M., Schoen, H., and Wuttke, A. (2018). Context-Driven Attitude Formation: The Difference Between Supporting Free Trade in the Abstract and Supporting Specific Trade Agreements. *Review of International Political Economy*, **25**(2), 215–42.

Jungherr, A., Posegga, O., and An, J. (2019a). Discursive Power in Contemporary Media Systems: A Comparative Framework. *The International Journal of Press/Politics*, **24**(4), 404–25.

Jungherr, A., Posegga, O., and An, J. (2021). Populist Supporters on Reddit: A Comparison of Content and Behavioral Patterns within Publics of Supporters of Donald Trump and Hillary Clinton. *Social Science Computer Review*. DOI: https://doi.org/10.1177/0894439321996130.

Jungherr, A., Rivero, G., and Gayo-Avello, D. (2020). *Retooling Politics: How Digital Media Are Shaping Democracy*. Cambridge: Cambridge University Press. DOI: https://doi.org/10.1017/9781108297820.

Jungherr, A., Schoen, H., and Jürgens, P. (2016). The Mediation of Politics through Twitter: An Analysis of Messages Posted during the Campaign for the German Federal Election 2013. *Journal of Computer-Mediated Communication*, **21**(1), 50–68.

Jungherr, A., Schoen, H., Posegga, O., and Jürgens, P. (2017). Digital Trace Data in the Study of Public Opinion: An Indicator of Attention Toward Politics Rather Than Political Support. *Social Science Computer Review*, **35**(3), 336–56.

Jungherr, A., and Schroeder, R. (2021). Disinformation and the Structural Transformations of the Public Arena: Addressing the Actual Challenges to Democracy. *Social Media + Society*, **7**(1), 1–13.

Jungherr, A., Schroeder, R., and Stier, S. (2019b). Digital Media and the Surge of Political Outsiders: Explaining the Success of Political Challengers in the United States, Germany, and China. *Social Media + Society*, **5**(3), 1–12.

Kahan, D. M., Peters, E., Wittlin, M., Slovic, P., Larrimore Ouellette, L., Braman, D., and Mandel, G. (2012). The Polarizing Impact of Science Literacy and Numeracy on Perceived Climate Change Risks. *Nature Climate Change*, **2**, 732–35.

Karl, J. (2020). *Front Row at the Trump Show*, New York: Dutton.

Karpf, D. (2016). *Analytical Activism: Digital Listerning and the New Political Strategy*. Oxford: Oxford University Press.

Kaye, D. (2019). *Speech Police: The Global Struggle to Govern the Internet*. New York: Columbia Global Reports.

Keller, D. (2018a). *Internet Platforms: Observations on Speech, Danger, and Money*. Stanford, CA: Hoover Institution. https://cyberlaw.stanford.edu/files/publication/files/381732092-internet-platforms-observations-on-speech-danger-and-money.pdf.

Keller, D. (2018b). The Right Tools: Europe's Intermediary Liability Laws and the EU 2016 General Data Protection Regulation. *Berkeley Technology Law Journal*, **33**(1), 287–364.

Keller, F. B., Schoch, D., Stier, S., and Yang, J. (2020). Political Astroturfing on Twitter: How to Coordinate a Disinformation Campaign. *Political Communication*, **37**(2), 256–80.

King, G., Pan, J., and Roberts, M. E. (2017). How the Chinese Government Fabricates Social Media Posts for Strategic Distraction, Not Engaged Argument. *American Political Science Review*, **111**(3), 484–501.

Kitchens, B., Johnson, S. L., and Gray, P. (2020). Understanding Echo Chambers and Filter Bubbles: The Impact of Social Media on Diversification and Partisan Shifts in News Consumption. *MIS Quarterly*, **44**(4), 1619–49.

Klonick, K. (2018). The New Governors: The People, Rules, and Processes Governing Online Speech. *Harvard Law Review*, **131**, 1598–670.

Kohrs, C. (2017). Russische propaganda für deutsche zuschauer. *Correctiv*. https://correctiv.org/aktuelles/neue-rechte/2017/01/04/russische-propaganda -fuer-deutsche-zuschauer/

Konieczna, M. (2018). *Journalism without Profit: Making News When the Market Fails*. Oxford: Oxford University Press.

Kostka, G. (2019). China's Social Credit Systems and Public Opinion: Explaining High Levels of Approval. *New Media & Society*, **21**(7), 1565–93.

Kovach, B., and Rosenstiel, T. (2021). *The Elements of Journalism: What Newspeople Should Know and the Public Should Expect*, 4th ed. New York: The Crown Publishing Group.

Kovic, M., Rauchfleisch, A., Sele, M., and Caspar, C. (2018). Digital Astroturfing in Politics: Definition, Typology, and Countermeasures. *Studies in Communication Sciences*, **18**(1), 69–85.

Kuhn, R., and Nielsen, R. K., eds. (2014). *Political Journalism in Transition: Western Europe in a Comparative Perspective*. London: I. B. Tauris.

Levin, Y. (2020). *A Time to Build: From Family and Community to Congress and the Campus, How Recommitting to Our Institutions Can Revive the American Dream*. New York: Basic Books.

Levitsky, S., and Ziblatt, D. (2018). *How Democracies Die*. New York: Crown Publishing Group.

Liang, F., Das, V., Kostyuk, N., and Hussain, M. M. (2018). Constructing a Data-Driven Society: China's Social Credit System as a State Surveillance Infrastructure. *Policy & Internet*, **10**(4), 415–53.

Lippman, W. (1928). *American Inquisitors*. New York: The Macmillan Company.

Liu, J. (2020). *Shifting Dynamics of Contention in the Digital Age: Mobile Communication and Politics in China*. Oxford: Oxford University Press.

Lowery, W. (2020). A Reckoning over Objectivity, Led by Black Journalists. *The New York Times*. https://www.nytimes.com/2020/06/23/opinion/objectiv ity-black-journalists-coronavirus.html

Lozada, C. (2020). *What Were We Thinking: A Brief Intellectual History of the Trump Era*. New York: Simon & Schuster.

Mann, M. (1986). *The Sources of Social Power*, vol. 1: *A History of Power from the Beginning to AD 1760*. Cambridge: Cambridge University Press.

Mann, M. (2013). *The Sources of Social Power*, vol. 4: *Globalizations, 1945–2011*. Cambridge: Cambridge University Press.

Mann, M., and Riley, D. (2006). Explaining Macro-regional Trends in Global Income Inequalities, 1950–2000. *Socio-Economic Review*, **5**(1), 81–115.

Maurer, M., Jost, P., Haßler, J., and Kruschinski, S. (2019). Auf den Spuren der Lügenpresse: Zur Richtigkeit und Ausgewogenheit der Medienberichterstattung in der "Flüchtlingskrise". *Publizistik*, **64**(1), 15–35.

McCarty, N., Poole, K. T., and Rosenthal, H. (2016). *Polarized America: The Dance of Ideology and Unequal Riches*, 2nd ed. Cambridge, MA: The MIT Press.

McCombs, M. E. (2014). *Setting the Agenda: Mass Media and Public Opinion*, 2nd ed. Cambridge: Polity Press.

McGregor, S. C. (2019). Social Media as Public Opinion: How Journalists Use Social Media to Represent Public Opinion. *Journalism*, **20**(8), 1070–86.

McGregor, S. C. (2020). "Taking the Temperature of the Room": How Political Campaigns Use Social Media to Understand and Represent Public Opinion. *Public Opinion Quarterly*, **84**(S1), 236–56.

McQuail, D. (2013). *Journalism and Society*. London: SAGE Publications.

Meyer, D. S., and Tarrow, S., eds. (2018). *The Resistance: The Dawn of the Anti-Trump Opposition Movement*. New York: Oxford University Press.

Miller-Idriss, C. (2020). *Hate in the Homeland: The New Global Far Right*. Princeton, NJ: Princeton University Press.

Napoli, P. M. (2019). *Social Media and the Public Interest: Media Regulation in the Disinformation Age*. New York: Columbia University Press.

Neuman, W. R. (2016). *The Digital Difference: Media Technology and the Theory of Communication Effects*. Cambridge, MA: Harvard University Press.

Neuman, W. R., Guggenheim, L., Jang, S. M., and Bae, S. Y. (2014). The Dynamics of Public Attention: Agenda-Setting Theory Meets Big Data. *Journal of Communication*, **64**(2), 193–214.

Newman, N., Fletcher, R., Schulz, A., Andı, S., and Nielsen, R. K., eds. (2020). *Reuters Institute Digital News Report 2020*. Oxford: Reuters Institute for the Study of Journalism.

Newman, N., Fletcher, R., Schulz, A., Andı, S., Robertson, C. T., and Nielsen, R. K., eds. (2021). *Reuters Institute Digital News Report 2021: 10th Edition*, Oxford: Reuters Institute for the Study of Journalism.

Nielsen, R. K. (2012). The Business of News. In T. Witschge, C. W. Anderson, D. Domingo, and A. Hermida, eds., *The SAGE Handbook of Digital Journalism*. London: SAGE Publications, 51–67.

Nielsen, R. K., and Ganter, S. A. (2018). Dealing with Digital Intermediaries: A Case Study of the Relations between Publishers and Platforms. *New Media & Society*, **20**(4), 1600–17.

Oreskes, N., and Conway, E. M. (2010). *Merchants of Doubt: How a Handful of Scientists Obscured the Truth on Issues from Tobacco Smoke to Global Warming*. New York: Bloomsbury Press.

Osnos, E. (2014). *Age of Ambition: Chasing Fortune, Truth, and Faith in the New China*. New York: Farrat, Straus; Giroux.

Palmer, D. A. (2019). Three Moral Codes and Microcivil Spheres in China. In J. C. Alexander, D. A. Palmer, S. Park, and A. S. Ku, eds., *The Civil Sphere in Asia*. New York: Cambridge University Press, 126–47.

Pan, J. (2017). How Market Dynamics of Domestic and Foreign Social Media Firms Shape Strategies of Internet Censorship. *Problems of Post-Communism*, **64**(3-4), 167–88.

Peck, R. (2019). *Fox Populism: Branding Conservatism as Working Class*. Cambridge: Cambridge University Press.

Pickard, V. (2020). *Democracy without Journalism? Confronting the Misinformation Society*. Oxford: Oxford University Press.

Pohle, J., and Thiel, T. (2020). Digital Sovereignty. *Internet Policy Review*, **9**(4), 1–19.

Posegga, O., and Jungherr, A. (2019). Characterizing Political Talk on Twitter: A Comparison between Public Agenda, Media Agendas, and the Twitter Agenda with Regard to Topics and Dynamics. In *HICSS 2019: Proceedings of the 52nd Hawaii International Conference on System Science*. University of Hawaii at Manoa: Scholarspace, 2590–99.

Przeworski, A. (2019). *Crises of Democracy*. Cambridge: Cambridge University Press.

Rauchfleisch, A. (2017). The Public Sphere as an Essentially Contested Concept: A Co-citation Analysis of the Last 20 Years of Public Sphere Research. *Communication and the Public*, **2**(1), 3–18.

Rauchfleisch, A., and Kaiser, J. (2020a). The False Positive Problem of Automatic Bot Detection in Social Science Research. *PLoS One*, **15**(10), e0241045.

Rauchfleisch, A., and Kaiser, J. (2020b). The German Far-Right on YouTube: An Analysis of User Overlap and User Comments. *Journal of Broadcasting & Electronic Media*, **64**(3), 373–96.

Rauchfleisch, A., and Kaiser, J. (2021). Deplatforming the Far-Right: An Analysis of YouTube and BitChute. *Social Science Research Network.* https://papers.ssrn.com/sol3/papers.cfm?abstract_id=3867818.

Rauchfleisch, A., and Schäfer, M. S. (2015). Multiple Public Spheres of Weibo: A Typology of Forms and Potentials of Online Public Spheres In China. *Information, Communication & Society*, **18**(2), 139–55.

Rekker, R. (2021). The Nature and Origins of Political Polarization over Science. *Public Understanding of Science*, **30**(4), 352–68.

Richardson, A. V. (2020). *Bearing Witness While Black: African Americans, Smartphones, and the New Protest #Journalism.* Oxford: Oxford University Press.

Rid, T. (2020). *Active Measures: The Secret History of Disinformation and Political Warfare.* New York: Farrat, Straus; Giroux.

Roberts, M. E. (2018). *Censored: Distraction and Diversion inside China's Great Firewall.* Princeton, NJ: Princeton University Press.

Robertson, C. T. (2021). Impartiality Unpacked: A Study of Four Countries. In N. Newman, R. Fletcher, A. Schulz, S. Andı, C. T. Robertson, and R. K. Nielsen, eds. *Reuters Institute Digital News Report 2021: 10th Edition.* Oxford: Reuters Institute for the Study of Journalism, 39–42.

Rodrik, D. (2011). *The Globalization Paradox: Democracy and the Future of the World Economy.* New York: W. W. Norton & Company.

Scharkow, M., Mangold, F., Stier, S., and Breuer, J. (2020). How Social Network Sites and Other Online Intermediaries Increase Exposure to News. *PNAS: Proceedings of the National Academy of Sciences of the United States of America*, **117**(6), 2761–63.

Schmidt, E., and Cohen, J. (2013). *The New Digital Age: Transforming Nations, Businesses, and Our Lives.* New York: Alfred A. Knopf.

Schroeder, R. (2013). *An Age of Limits: Social Theory for the 21st Century.* Basingstoke: Palgrave Macmillan.

Schroeder, R. (2018a). Rethinking Digital Media and Political Change. *Convergence*, **24**(2), 168–83.

Schroeder, R. (2018b). *Social Theory after the Internet: Media, Technology and Globalization.* London: UCL Press.

Schroeder, R. (2019). Contemporary Populist Politics through the Macroscopic Lens of Randall Collins's Conflict Theory. *Thesis Eleven*, **154**(1), 97–107.

Schroeder, R. (2020). Political Power and the Globalizing Spread of Populist Politics. *Journal of Political Power*, **13**(1), 22–40.

Scott, M., Bunce, M., and Wright, K. (2019). Foundation Funding and the Boundaries of Journalism. *Journalism Studies*, **20**(14), 2034–52.

Sehl, A., Simon, F. M., and Schroeder, R. (2020). The Populist Campaigns against European Public Service Media: Hot Air or Existential Threat? *International Communication Gazette.*

Settle, J. E. (2018). *Frenemies: How Social Media Polarizes America.* Cambridge: Cambridge University Press.

Shoemaker, P. J., and Reese, S. D. (2014). *Mediating the Message in the 21st Century,* 3rd ed. New York: Routledge.

Shoemaker, P. J., and Vos, T. P. (2009). *Gatekeeping Theory.* New York: Routledge.

Sides, J., Tesler, M., and Vavreck, L. (2018). *Identity Crisis: The 2016 Presidential Campaign and the Battle for the Meaning of America.* Princeton, NJ: Princeton University Press.

Skocpol, T., and Tervo, C. (Eds.). (2020). *Upending American Politics: Polarizing Parties, Ideological Elites, and Citizen Activists from the Tea Party to the Anti-Trump Resistance.* New York: Oxford University Press.

Slater, D., and Wong, J. (2013). The Strength to Concede: Ruling Parties and Democratization in Developmental Asia. *Perspectives on Politics,* **11**(3), 717–33.

Smith, R. M., and King, D. (2020). White Protectionism in America. *Perspectives on Politics,* **19**(2), 460–78.

Sobieraj, S. (2020). *Credible Threat: Attacks against Women Online and the Future of Democracy.* Oxford: Oxford University Press.

Stier, S., Kirkizh, N., Froio, C., and Schroeder, R. (2020). Populist Attitudes and Selective Exposure to Online News: A Cross-Country Analysis Combining Web Tracking and Surveys. *The International Journal of Press/Politics,* **25**(3), 426–46.

Stier, S., Posch, L., Bleier, A., and Strohmaier, M. (2017). When Populists become Popular: Comparing Facebook Use by the Right-Wing Movement Pegida and German Political Parties. *Information, Communication & Society,* **20**(9), 1365–88.

Stockmann, D. (2013). *Media Commercialization and Authoritarian Rule in China.* Cambridge: Cambridge University Press.

Stockmann, D. (2020). Regulating Social Media Platforms: Lessons from China for Europe. In *Digital Democracy Workshop,* Digital Democracy Lab & Digital Society Initiative, University of Zurich.

Stockmann, D., and Luo, T. (2017). Which Social Media Facilitate Online Public Opinion in China? *Problems of Post-Communism,* **64**(3–4), 189–202.

Stockmann, D., Luo, T., and Shen, M. (2020). Designing Authoritarian Deliberation: How Social Media Platforms Influence Political Talk in China. *Democratization,* **27**(2), 243–63.

Strittmatter, K. (2018). *Die neuerfindung der diktatur: Wie china den digitalen Überwachungsstaat aufbaut und uns damit herausfordert.* Munich: Piper.

Strossen, N. (2018). *Hate: Why we Should Resist It with Free Speech, Not Censorship.* Oxford: Oxford University Press.

Sunstein, C. R. (2017). *#Republic: Divided Democracy in the Age of Social Media.* Princeton, NJ: Princeton University Press.

Suzor, N. P. (2019). *Lawless: The Secret Rules That Govern Our Digital Lives.* Cambridge: Cambridge University Press.

Taneja, H., Wu, A. X., and Edgerly, S. (2018). Rethinking the Generational Gap in Online News Use: An Infrastructural Perspective. *New Media & Society,* **20**(5), 1792–812.

Tang, W. (2016). *Populist Authoritarianism: Chinese Political Culture and Regime Stability.* New York, NY: Oxford University Press.

Termin, P. (2017). *The Vanishing Middle Class: Prejudice and Power in a Dual Economy.* Cambridge, MA: The MIT Press.

Theocharis, Y., Barberá, P., Fazekas, Z., Popa, S. A., and Parnet, O. (2016). A Bad Workman Blames His Tweets: The Consequences of Citizens' Uncivil Twitter Use When Interacting with Party Candidates. *Journal of Communication,* **66**(6), 1007–31.

Theocharis, Y., and Jungherr, A. (2021). Computational Social Science and the Study of Political Communication. *Political Communication,* **38**(1–2), 1–22.

Toepfl, F., and Piwoni, E. (2018). Targeting Dominant Publics: How Counterpublic Commenters Align Their Efforts with Mainstream News. *New Media & Society,* **20**(5), 2011–27.

Toff, B., Badrinathan, S., Mont'Alverne, C., Arguedas, A. R., Fletcher, R., and Nielsen, R. K. (2021). *Listening to What Trust in News Means to Users: Qualitative Evidence from Four Countries.* Oxford: Reuters Institute for the Study of Journalism. https://reutersinstitute.politics.ox.ac.uk/sites/default/files/2021-04/Toff_et_al_Listening_to_What_Trust_in_News_Means_to_Users_FINAL.pdf.

Usher, N. (2017). Digital Journalism Venture-Backed News Startups and the Field of Journalism. *Journalism,* **5**(9), 1116–33.

Vargo, C. J., Guo, L., and Amazeen, M. A. (2018). The Agenda-Setting Power of Fake News: A Big Data Analysis of the Online Media Landscape from 2014 to 2016. *New Media & Society,* **20**(5), 2028–49.

Wahl-Jorgensen, K., Berry, M., Garcia-Blanco, I., Bennett, L., and Cable, J. (2017). Rethinking Balance and Impartiality in Journalism? How the BBC Attempted and Failed to Change the Paradigm. *Journalism,* **18**(7), 781–800.

Waisbord, S. (2020). Mob Censorship: Online Harassment of US Journalists in Times of Digital Hate and Populism. *Digital Journalism,* **8**(8), 1030–46.

Wang, J. (2020). *Regulation of Digital Media Platforms: The Case of China.* Oxford: The Foundation for Law, Justice; Society. https://www.fljs.org/content/regulation-digital-media-platforms-case-china

Warner, M. (2002). *Publics and Counterpublics.* New York: Zone Books.

Webster, J. G. (2014). *The Marketplace of Attention: How Audiences Take Shape in a Digital Age.* Cambridge, MA: The MIT Press.

Weiß, V. (2017). *Die autoritäre revolte: Die neue rechte und der untergang des abendlandes.* Stuttgart: Klett-Cotta.

Whyte, M. K. (2010). *Myth of the Social Volcano: Perceptions of Inequality and Distributive Injustice in Contemporary China.* Stanford, CA: Stanford University Press.

Wiedeman, R. (2020). Times Change. *New York Magazine.* https://nymag.com/intelligencer/2020/11/inside-the-new-york-times-heated-reckoning-with-itself.html

Wright, T. (2018). *Popular Protest in China.* Cambridge: Polity Press.

Wright, T., ed. (2019). *Handbook of Protest and Resistance in China.* Cheltenham: Edward Elgar Publishing.

Yan, P., and Schroeder, R. (2020). Variations in the Adoption and Use of Mobile Social Apps in Everyday Lives in Urban and Rural China. *Mobile Media & Communication,* **8**(3), 318–41.

Yang, T., Majó-Vásquez, S., Nielsen, R. K., and González-Bailón, S. (2020). Exposure to News Grows Less Fragmented with an Increase in Mobile Access. *PNAS: Proceedings of the National Academy of Sciences of the United States of America,* **117**(46), 28678–83.

Zhao, D. (2009). The Mandate of Heaven and Performance Legitimation in Historical and Contemporary China. *American Behavioral Scientist,* **53**(3), 416–33.

Zhu, Y., and Fu, K. (2020). Speaking Up or Staying Silent? Examining the Influences of Censorship and Behavioral Contagion on Opinion (Non-) Expression in China. *New Media & Society.* DOI: https://doi.org/10.1177/1461444820959016.

Zuckerman, E., and Rajendra-Nicolucci, C. (2021). Deplatforming Our Way to the Alt-Tech Ecosystem: What Happens When You Exile Users and Communities? *Knight First Amendment Institute at Columbia University.* https://knightcolumbia.org/blog/deplatforming-our-way-to-the-alt-tech-ecosystem.

Acknowledgments

Although this is a very short Element, we accrued considerable intellectual debt along the way. Many friends and colleagues inspired, encouraged, and corrected us along the way. We thank Matthew S. Erie, Caterina Froio, Valeska Gerstung, Marlies von der Malsburg, Anne Schulz, Felix Simon, Sebastian Stier, Thomas Streinz, Yannis Theocharis, and Pu Yan for critically engaging with our arguments and generously providing comments. We also thank Stuart Soroka, editor of the Cambridge Elements series "Politics and Communication" for his support of the Element and his guidance through the publishing process. We thank two anonymous reviewers who critically engaged with the draft of this Element. The final product is better for all this gracious support and engagement.

Cambridge Elements $\equiv$

Politics and Communication

Stuart Soroka

University of California

Stuart Soroka is Professor in the Department of Communication at the University of California, Los Angeles, and Adjunct Research Professor at the Center for Political Studies at the Institute for Social Research, University of Michigan. His research focuses on political communication, political psychology, and the relationships between public policy, public opinion, and mass media. His books with Cambridge University Press include *The Increasing Viability of Good News* (2021, with Yanna Krupnikov), *Negativity in Democratic Politics* (2014), *Information and Democracy* (forthcoming, with Christopher Wlezien) and *Degrees of Democracy* (2010, with Christopher Wlezien).

About the Series

Cambridge Elements in Politics and Communication publishes research focused on the intersection of media, technology, and politics. The series emphasizes forward-looking reviews of the field, path-breaking theoretical and methodological innovations, and the timely application of social-scientific theory and methods to current developments in politics and communication around the world.

Cambridge Elements ≡

Politics and Communication

.

Printed in the United States
by Baker & Taylor Publisher Services